AF577151

Other books

by Kay Magenheimer

LOVE'S STIGMATA

BORN AGAIN

Signed for my friend,
Mrs. Arthur Anderson
Kay Magenheimer
December 7, 199[illegible]

FIRST LIGHT TO DAWN

Dear Bere,
Our memories
in the life of the
spirit go back
a long, long time.
I love you.
Kay

Photo by Jacqueline Pailleret

Kay Magenheimer

at the Paris Bookstalls

1961

at 53

FIRST LIGHT TO DAWN

A Collection of Poems

in Three Parts

by

KAY MAGENHEIMER

Foreword by Eugenia Price

Runnymede Press

Carrollton, Georgia

Published by Runnymede Press
Carrollton, Georgia

AUTHOR'S NOTE

Selections have been previously published in *Abba Babba* in 1991; *Born Again* in 1977 and *Love's Stigmata* in 1963 and copyright renewed in 1991. Other poems have been published over the years in numerous publications.

Library of Congress Catalog Card No. 92-085139

ISBN 0-9634972-0-0

Printed in the United States of America

Foreword

It has been said that "poetry is a synthesis of hyacinths and biscuits."

I forget who said it. A poet, I'm sure. And it is conclusive, yet also inconclusive—not enough. Only poetry itself can describe or even intimate poetry: what it is. *What it really is.*

I would never try to define it. Having written poetry myself in my youth (still wishing I had the time to try it now that I am no longer young) I revere it too much to attempt a definition. Perhaps there is none. Poetry is the sturdy stake in the ground; it is also more gossamer than the bright tail of a sunset or an insect wing. True it is made of the hyacinth's fragrance (even that of a blue hyacinth, my favorite).

Poetry is also biscuits—food. Both are called to mind when, on those rare occasions, one finds true poetry.

My beloved, longtime friend, Kay Magenheimer, writes true poetry.

Not once does she ignore either hyacinths or biscuits.

Here in these pages you will find both pouring from her poet's heart—the heart of spirit, of Spirit, of love, of sorrow, humor, joy and sheer wonder at the essence of God and all He created. All He redeemed. All He longs to redeem.

I write these lines in a time of ugliness in the world: A time when hideous, needless pain and strife slash at the hearts of people and at the heart of God. Certainly at my heart. You will find healing here, as you read. I found it.

Perhaps earlier I've written a Foreword for some other book of poems I don't now remember, but none which points as does this one, to the essence of the word *poem*. The word too often used to mask mere rhyme, awkward verse. Kay Magenheimer captures the untellable "synthesis of hyacinths and biscuits." And more.

These are real poems. Kay is a poet. Read her. Once you do, you will read her again and again and bring to her poems the needs and the insights of your own mind's heart as she has brought hers.

Eugenia Price
St. Simons Island, Georgia

For

members of my family

and friends who gave so generously

of their time and labor

to help me construct this book

Foreword by Eugenia Price *vii*
Afterword *xxxvi*

Contents

Part I
First Light

Love's Stigmata 1
A Crocus Out of Season 3
Winter 5
Condolence to a Very Old Man on the Death of His Wife 6
To Hear an Old Man Tell It 7
Before TV 8
"I Will Not Leave You Orphans" 9
Columbine-Child at Midnight 11
How Difficult the Old? 13
Mental Breakdown 14
Anger 15
1776 - 1963 16
White to Black 17
Transients All 21
Yevtushenko 22
Cuban Exiles 23
De Gaulle 25
Truman 27
Eleanor Roosevelt 28

"Ask Not . . . " 29
Memory at Bladon 31
Jason Leaves Home 33
November 22 - Two Years Later 34
Konrad Adenauer 35
Toward Freedom 37
Desolate Night 38
Immolation of a President 39
The General Must Sleep 41
Between Hawk and Buzzard 43
For Bachelors 45
Even Today 46
Of All Seasons 47
Love Was Ever a Rainbow 49
The Same Thing As It Was Told
in a Different World 50
Incompatibility 51
The Importance of Touch 52
Unexpected Happening 53
The Wife of a Nightworker 54
Alaskan Heritage 55
"If I Had at Least Enriched the Earth . . ." 59
"Let Him Have Dominion" 60
Man! Know What I Mean, Man? 61
Mother-Earth 63
A Poet Contemplates
a Rejection Slip 64
Robert Moses 65
Sleep Well 67

Unhinged in Our Time 68
Death Comes with Soft Laughter 69
An Irish Mother 71
The Jeweled Crown 74
A Prerevolutionary Teacher 76
Love Is Inscrutable 77
What Is the Name of Pain? 78
The Young Speeder 79
Sounds Heard
with Early Morning Coffee 81
The *Santa Maria*,
the *Niña*, and the *Pinta* 83
El Salvador 84
Mistaken Identity 85
Pascula Florida 86
Mississippi River 87
Waterie Labyrinth 88
Can the Cocoon Hold
a Butterfly Forever? 90
From This Time On 92
Environment for Retirement 95
Conception 98
What Is in a Name? 100
Laurraine Goreau 102
A Meeting Between Old Friends 104
In a Rose Garden 107
Intrusion 108
Seven New Moons for Uranus 109

Roy Wilkins at Hyde Park 111
Golda Meir 114
Iran, O Negligent Mother! 116
A Light Goes Out in Egypt 118
The Nuclear Beasts 120
The Toad, Remembering, Hides His Head 122
Whips and Chains 126
O Earth!
When Will Your Tent Be in Peace? 127
This Way! 129
But One Reason for
Writing Poems for the Dead 133
A Canterbury Bell 135
Divergent Sisters 139
A Fairy Tale 146
A Four-Months-Old Fetus
Carried Across Campus
in a Plastic Bag 151
A Golden Gift 153
Joseph Edward Carlson 156
Heat Wave in Georgia 157
The Generator 160
Grainne 161
Kinship 163
Moon-Walker and Her Mother 165
The Maypole 168
My Angel Shall Go Before You 169
Night Intruders 173

Observing Samuel Beckett
Observe an Old Couple 175
On Reading Certain—
Not *All*, Thank God!—
Love Poems of Rod McKuen 179
The Drug Addict and His Mother 181
Lament 182
P'an-Ku, Confucius,
and the Modern World 183
Lauren 187
A Poet Makes a Poem 188
Genie and St. Simons Island 191
Without Tears 192
Remarks on Friendships
and on Ours 194
A Valentine for Carrollton 200
Snow Drifting 202
The Widowed Mother and the Virgin 204
Mary Payne Williams 207
To Each His Own 208
The Watering-Hole 210
Wind Song 216
A Toast to a Bride-to-be 217
My Guardian Angel 219

Part II

Cloud of the Unknown

Legacy of Sappho 222
How It Started 223
The Return Gift 224
Psyche Uncertain 226
Ah! Be Still a Moment 228
Prescience 229
Numbness 230
There Is No More Wine 231
Greenwich Village 232
The Gay Spot 236
C'est Paris 238
"Every time I cross the Seine, I think of you . . ." 240
The Open Wound 241
From the Cross 242
That Which You Have 244
The Golden Ring 246
A Season Between 247
I Bring You a Cherry 248
I Love You 249
Irresolute 250
Love Is Joy 251
Bargain in Zanzibar 252
For Laura 253
A Robber in Corinth 254
Nolle Prosequi 255

There Are Some 256
What You Mean to Me 257
Are You Adverse to Me?
Or Averse to Me? 258
Grapes of Pink Wax 260
A Single Yellow Rose 264
Some There Are
Who Live the Lord's Last Passover 266
We Reap What We Sow 268
When Dreams Explode in Smoke 270
That Which You Made, You Know 272
Celebration for Judy 274
Golden Were Her Hands 276
Love's Homecoming 279
. . . sans everything 280
The Irony of Dreams 282
Friendship 285
My Sole Gift 286
Once in a Cool, Green Wood 288
Rejuvenescence 290
Renoir Woman 294
A Time of Joy 296
There Being Times When . . . 297
For This There Is No Name 298
A Fragrance Escaped From Heaven 300
A Day and a Night in a Special Sea 301
Where Are You, My Love? 302

Part III

Dawn

Born Again 303
John XXIII 307
An Ecumenical Protest 308
Portrait of a Nun 309
Benediction at Ladyrock 311
Christmas Comes *Every Year* to an Unhappy World 313
Star-Crossed 315
Urbi et Orbi 316
A Rosary Falls in Surprise 318
Anniversary Mass for My Mother 320
A Benedictine Monk on a Georgia Battlefield 321
The Jews 335
Celebrate the Christ 337
Defraud Not the Widow of Her Sorrow 338
The Donkey and the Woman 341
Early Came the Magdalene 343
Feed My Lambs 345
From Intimate Impulse 348
Full of Amazement 351
Here Am I, Lord 353
. . . I Give Unto You 356
On This Holy Night 357
Jacob's Ladder 358
A Pope from Poland 365

Jesus! Emmanuel! 366
Joseph 368
Joseph, Follow Me! 370
The King of Israel 372
To the Mother of Heaven
for the Children of Earth 374
Let Thy Light
Rise Up in the Darkness 375
The Lonely Albatross 381
The Lord Is Risen,
as the Women Said 383
My Beloved Son 385
My Stones Cry Out to You 389
A Song to God 393
Stand Still! Turn Around
and Look at Me! 395
Throne of Christ 396
The Unconverted 398
When Death Is Ecstasy 399
An Unexpected Trip to Bethlehem 402
We Know You by Your Name 404
Woman and the First Christmas 408
The Divine Bargain 411
Peter to Paul VI 412
†Thomas and His Knights 415
His Presence 418
Balancing Accounts 420
Is Man to Dominate Heaven Too? 422

A Letter to Paul 429
Women Throughout the Ages 432
The Question 436
Abba Baba 438
Et Homo Factus Est . . . Passus 440
The Garden of Gethsemane 443
Growing Old 445

Photo by Ellison Driscoll

KM in Babylon, New York

1963

at 55

Part I

FIRST LIGHT

(Perception—the Stirring of the Intellect)

To the memory of

my beloved parents

Henry and Marie (*née* Thiele) Magenheimer

LOVE'S STIGMATA

Her little wordless cries,
Rapier-thin against his breast,
Pierced his heart as truly
As the needle to the pole.

Primeval in its twisting and turning,
Luminous as a star flung into space
By a love-making god,
Her body—

Long after his touch
Had found its lodestar—
Convulsively, gradually
Settled down to a quiet peace.

His thoughts created her as his hand had.
He was a god; and looking at her,
He found her good.
He said then "I love you."

But once—
Before him—
She had tasted the fruit
That had been forbidden her.

Now, driven to cover
The nakedness of her remembrance,
She cried to him: "Don't! Don't say
'I love you.' "
And hid her face from the divine fire.

In sorrow, then, they lost
The Eden they had shared;
And he turned his back upon her
To weep over the mystery of creation.

But so he loves her
Or remembered the grace
That was upon her in Paradise,
He stretched out his hand to her.

Swiftly, incredibly, she pressed it
Deep into her breast,
Subconsciously seeking redemption
By nailing him to her flesh.

But spikes leave wounds
That do not close;
And another—reaching for his hand—
Will surely notice these scars.

A CROCUS OUT OF SEASON

Unexpectedly, she came like a soft day
in spring
When, having felt a bitter chill in the air,
He was hurriedly harvesting
Against the long night of his soul's winter.

He burned then all that he had sowed;
And, as if it were March, he plowed again
his field,
Giving no thought to the snow
Down-drafting on the breath of the wind.

For when she came,
A gold and blue crocus
Sprang up under the untamed
Tardy tree of his heart.

Who is there who can suddenly find
A crocus out of season
And not be aware of springtime?
And its sweet, trembling promise?

He should have remembered, after she
    had gone—
How penetrating this wind, this cold!—
The reason for wilted fronds
And worn-out lady's slippers;

That spring flowers are too frail
To dare a heart more than for the moment—
How soon they grow pale
Before its wondrous, wondering fire.

Somehow, it kept slipping
His memory
That—even in spring—
A crocus

Is not meant to have the strength
Nor the stamina to withstand
The scorching heat of summer—
Let alone winter's icy breath.

WINTER

Things die in winter
When chill icy blasts
Blow out of the North.
Trees mourn with their aching arms
Stretched toward the skies.
Gone is the warm sunshine,
The singing birds.
Gone, too, is the laughter
Of small children.
Snow—
Grieving Nature's frozen tears—
Adorns with white crystals,
And kindness,
The insensible earth.

CONDOLENCE TO A VERY OLD MAN ON THE DEATH OF HIS WIFE

. . . when I found my voice,
I asked him
Didn't he want to sit down?

TO HEAR AN OLD MAN TELL IT

The old man has the snow
Piled so high now, he doesn't realize
He has added a foot to it
Every year since he was five.

The 75th Anniversary of the Blizzard of '88:
March 11, 1963

BEFORE TV

With a penny whistle
And an ear for the music
Of the wild sea and the wild woods,
He was

The story-teller—
The beloved Pied Piper—
Of our bewitched,
Charm-engirdled childhood.

For my Father

"I WILL NOT LEAVE YOU ORPHANS"*

For my Mother and my Father
June 25, 1960—February 22, 1961

A flourish of trumpets was in his voice,
In his hearty hello and his happy goodbye.
He, who had no choice of movement, had
his choice
At last with a sigh.

For years a gay prisoner of his bed,
He had gone to seek my mother with that sigh.
Impulsive in life, in death he still will have
his head:
With *ho* and a *hie*

He will greet her and with a great noise demand
of her
What took her so long—seven, almost eight
months—
To get their new home ready for them?
"I took time because

The sound of your joyous laughter filled
my ears
And your room at once; and the songs
you sang
Sparkled the eyes of the saints
And those who missed me."

An earthling still, all at once I felt sharply bereft,
Like a lost child who cannot find his mother
in a crowd.
Bewildered, alone, I held
My face in my hands.

When suddenly—oh! the swift consolation
of God.
The filling of the emptiness!—I thought:
This skin I touch is her skin,
The skin she made

While I lay loved—unafraid—in the house
of her womb.
This is her skin, her bones, *their* blood
That pumps through my heart—the heart
Their love provided.

The dead are not dead. They live!
They are as close
As the hand is on the face.

*St. John 14:18

COLUMBINE-CHILD AT MIDNIGHT

Quiet as a bird
Sleeping in its nest
With a dream feathered
Under its purple vest,

I, Harlequin—
Unmasked but strangely happy—
Sensed her near;
And put down my book to see

The sun at the witching hour
Skipping a child's
Rope in her
Sparkling, blue blue eyes;

While her guardian angel
Held a golden
Buttercup
Close under her seashell chin.

Oh! Guileless Innocence
Clutching ragged dolls—
Your eyes
Twinkling like hyacinth stars—

By what mischievous pixie
Were you enticed
To give me this
Moment of delight?

For my two-year-old grandniece,
Mary Beth Germinario

HOW DIFFICULT THE OLD?

At the sound of his bell
I would fly—
In the middle of the night—
To his room

To find his need
Was to share with someone
The white light of the night
Falling like a soft veil over the rose garden.

"Look at the moon!"
And his voice trembled with wonder
At the beauty of the world
Turned bride at midnight.

I would touch his hand then,
Guessing at the memories
That were locked
In his wrinkled, bedridden heart.

For my Father

MENTAL BREAKDOWN

Her egotism
And the cast of her mind
Conspired to this confusion.

Friends and God,
Confounded and shut out
By the clamor
Of her insistence,
Wait patiently
For a sign of grace.

But
True to her imprint—
Not now being able
To hear any but her own voice—
She feeds her self-pity
On imagined abandonment
And bangs at the gate of a living hell
For the ultimatum.

ANGER

The expression of anger is as varied
    as personality;
Yet an artificial world will accept but one:
The one that holds the head up with a splint,
Covering our eyes with a hard, opaque chiten.

The disparaging gesture that tells the truth
Or a voice that thunders with the flash
Of lightning in its eyes
Are, they say, uncivilized and to be despised.

But honest anger is both a trauma and traumatic.
It purges the spirit, compelling a quick
    forgiveness;
While a head so vainly held as fashion decrees
Holds forever the sickness of our frailties.

1776—1963

Oh! Birmingham's shame!
Metamorphosing
The *eagle*—freedom's
Symbol, the hope of
The poor and oppressed—
Into a vicious
Snarling *dog* snapping
At defenseless men:
The dark despair of
Lovers of justice
Everywhere; the joy
Of gleeful despots
Clapping bloody hands
Over bully *Bulls*.

WHITE TO BLACK

Ah! Black man!
The intensity of you
Absorbing all the colors
Of the sun.

Ebony woman!
Cinderella of the race!—
The bottom
Of Pandora's box—

Your heart
Hopes with the desire
Of an ancient Jewess
To give birth to the Christ

Who would lead
Your people out of slavery,
To freedom
Under God, under man.

Not freedom
To live insecurely
In poverty
Among whites and unwanted,

But a guaranty
To be safe;
Accepted;
To wear the seal of humanity.

A Christ who would lead you
To true independence
Unchained not only,
But also unimpeded
To find

Your place in the sun;
And your sons,
Released from bonds,
To grow mightily in spirit.

You are not to blame
How would you know—
Without education?—
Of our struggle

For liberty;
Our rebellion
Against white chains,
Suppression and hindrance?

This was the lot
Of powerless men
From their distant beginning
Until less than

A century
Before your liberation,
We declared ourselves
Free from kings

And lords to whom
Our fathers were serfs,
Bound even to the right
Of the bride's night;

From kings who held
Men's hearts by empty hope
When they would not
By real satisfaction.

We know,
As you will discover,
That fully free, no man dwells
In painless towers.

None but God
Can boast of true freedom,
And even He is stymied
By Man's free will.

As we were, you are: Miserably
Exposed
To torture of the spirit,
To pain.

Alas! We are now
Far removed
From the injustices that made us
Break our bonds;

And we have forgotten
Pain and hunger
And the brutal chains
That bound our hearts.

Foolish pride
In our achievements
Has turned our heads from you,
Our hearts from God,

Who made Man
With the same variety,
The same essence
As all His creation.

This pride nullifies
Our gifts.
Free us. Oh! *Free us*, Black Brothers,
Before we die.

TRANSIENTS ALL

Even as we . . .
With stretched Pain they were won,
These souls bound by multicolored skins;
Or un-understanding.

Deaf, destructive, ice-veined
Are those who can't see
That—dead or alive—we all bow
The same distance from God.

YEVTUSHENKO

The Russian poet knows,
He knows and weeps
Because a Jew must again be crucified.

He weeps, he suffers
Because a Jew must again be crucified
In Russia.

The word shocks . . .
Then caresses the heart with a promise:
Russia will love again.

CUBAN EXILES

Cuba! A comely youth, wearer
Of the magic girdle.
Nutbrown
Hair

And cinnamon eyes caught
Aborning
In a shower of gold
By warm emerald water.

Cuba, poor poor Cuba
Lies dead now
In a copper sea—
Wounded by a wild boar

Who led him the
Long mountainous chase
After
Batista:

Flashing, in a black beard, a gleaming
Sinister smile—Hera's shield—
Bearing the date of Cuba's demise,
The twenty-sixth of July.

But from where he lies
There has sprung
From his blood
Anemone exiles—

Virile plants,
Shaken but not destroyed by hostile winds—
Whose memories will awaken
Their perished Adonis.

They are his promise
Of spring and winter,
And the seasons between—
His grieving mother, his brothers

Waiting,
With fern seed
On their leaves,
To hear him sing.

DE GAULLE

His self-respect
They call his pride.
Pride in his country
Is named conceit.

His self-assurance,
Haughtiness;
More—arrogance,
In their peddler's French.

Forgotten
Is a wounded France
And a feathered bird
Folding his wings about her;

Dropping fleur-de-lis
From his beak
To revive her to who she was
And might yet be.

He rides swiftly
Now on a silver arrow
Through savage air
To guard her destiny.

No timid *L'Aiglon* he,
But a mighty eagle
Soaring out of sight
Alone, courageously.

Pride of country
Is his pride;
That bears
No effrontry

To Clovic blood's remembrance
Of the Roman sun that rose
Above the Alps
On Provence;

And—centuries before Caesar—
Of sailor Greeks
Who, dropping wooden anchors,
Left at Marseille their shining Massalia.

TRUMAN

Cock-a-hoop at eighty,
His vernal, aweless heart
Outwits his loved Eos

Into granting age to
Become a sceptre in
His hands; and his humor,

His faithfulness, golden
Epaulets for his suit
Of immortality.

For the Honorable Harry S Truman
President of the United States
1945-1953

On his eightieth birthday.

A still from a home movie

*Eleanor Roosevelt and Kay Magenheimer**

at Val Kill

1955

**at 47*

ELEANOR ROOSEVELT

It was said—it was true—
She was a gabbler and a gadabout,
Gainsaying
Her diffidence.

Who then could foresee
In nineteen thirty-three
That this gaberlunyie for experience
Would become a mendicant for independence,
Carrying emeralds and gold
In her pouch
For the oppressed;
And, under her gabardine cloak,
A bowl of rice,
A loaf of bread
For the hungry.

August 1955
After a visit with E.R. at Val Kill

To Kay – God love you
Richard Cardinal Cushing +

John Fitzgerald Kennedy

President of the United States
1961—1963

"ASK NOT . . . "*

IN MEMORY OF
JOHN FITZGERALD KENNEDY

"No man while I live
And behold light on earth
Shall lay violent hands on thee"**
My country, my liberty.

Grieving unspeakably
For all creation;
For his country's sake, for dying liberty
And our children's unseen fate,

This man . . . this beacon for humanity . . .
With heart cast of oak and daring,
Made his great resolve
And nailed his colors to the mast.

Above the thunder of the wild sea
Breaking against his bleak New England coast,
His voice rose to shake the mighty halls of earth,
To rouse men from their sleep.

So little time for Hera's charge;
So short, so short a time for glory,
As if some great maternal Thetis
Had foretold this immortal story:

Our mighty Achilles lies dead
In the arms of his gallant Love,
Slain by some malignant spirit
Before the victory's claimed.

Rise up! Rise up, America!
Before it is too late.
His young, strong hand no longer
Shields us from an evil fate.

The only hand that can save us
Is the One he held . . . as his son held his.
America! America! Awake!
Before it is too late.

*From President Kennedy's Inaugural Address:
Ask not what your country can do for you.
Ask what you can do for your country.
**From *The Iliad* of Homer.

Written on the date of burial:
November 25, 1963

MEMORY AT BLADON

Hear! O! Hear me!
London! Liverpool!
The earth is refugee
From no April fool.

Hear! Englishmen!
The irritated air.
Poet! Wherrymen!
Beware! Beware!

The earth is sport
Of weighty boots.
On! On to the sally port!
Or freedom, tyranny uproots.

* * * * *

A floundering Ship of State
Piped him aboard
Peace in our time to execrate;
And flashed to a navy oared:

Winston is back!

To become
The stayer, the sender
Of bombs from Cockneydom;
Dogged protector

Of the city, its monuments,
Its streets . . .
And defence
Of villages and meadows-sweet;

A cable of courage and power
To pull Britain's
Own through their darkest hour
More hopeless then than Anne Boleyn's.

To become the patriarch
In his ancient years,
The beloved seamark
Of a world again and again in tears . . .

But what sacrifice the dead, the sweat?
Men their brothers yet destroy, enslave, abase
In Biafra, Viet Nam, in Baltimore . . .
To his unconquered spirit,
Forgotten, ignored their debt—
Acknowledged once—at his Bladon grave.

In tribute to
The Savior of Britain:
Sir Winston Churchill, K.G.
Dead January 24, 1965

JASON LEAVES HOME

Armed men spring up here and there from
Dragons' teeth he had to sow
In relentless search for the golden peace.

Who will destroy these doomsday men
Aware of his lifeless limbs
Lying under a London chimney-piece?

O Medea-World! Loving him,
Yours was the heart's sole power
To secure for him his desired fleece.

By his seed, rich in his spirit,
Are your children, fearful now
Of their mother. Pity your progeny!

Wreak not your spiteful vengeance
Now that he has deserted you
For lovelier, younger Eternity.

For Adlai E. Stevenson
U.S. Ambassador to the U.N.
Died July 14, 1965

NOVEMBER 22—TWO YEARS LATER

What would he say, he say?
What would say this bonhomie
From the nether side of Mandalay
About our Great Society?

Is this what he gave his life for:
That we should be secure
From the cradle to the grave and, therefore,
Rendered again a people immature?

Was it for draft cards burned?
And self-immolation of Americans—
Not Buddhists—but Americans unconcerned
By a child's countenance:

His John-John's, your John—
To both of whom he left his spirit,
Crossed his Rubicon,
And asked not what he might acquit?

In memoriam
President John F. Kennedy
Dead November 22, 1963

KONRAD ADENAUER

"High nosed was he and highboned of face.
Never did he lose heart, and
Of naught was he afraid . . . "*

His mighty sword of Faith
His only armor;
Needful indeed

To assay the monster
Spewing poison
From its foul, dank cave.

As might have been foretold:
From across the seas
Came good men with lances bold

To expose, at last,
To Siegfried's sword,
Evil unsurpassed.

Then lay the dragon dead—
The dreaded worm of the flat,
The evil-looking head.

Not so, in detail,
The burning memory
Of its cruel, bone-crushing tail.

Now it was decreed that, unarmed,
Only he without fear
Could pass, unhurt, unharmed,

Through the flaming hatred
Of a world bereft,
To find his slumbering Brünnhilde;

To reawaken
His country's conscience,
Ignominiously forsaken.

Mindful of the tainted air,
He was courageous of duty, and
Ever watchful in deed and prayer.

Nor will it ever be forgot
How Death found him, old and faithful still,
Under the Crag of the Dragon's Rock.

For Dr. Konrad Adenauer
Architect and First President
Republic of West Germany
Died April 19, 1967

*From the Legend of Siegfried
in the *Nibelungenlied*.

TOWARD FREEDOM

Dead, dead lies Liberty's son—
A paradox to those who could not,
Would not understand.
Now the dastardly deed is done
Even as he reached the Promised Land.

Mourning with shocked compassion
His young, his bloody sacrifice,
In one dread moment—fearful, ashen—
We bow to justice, to his urgent advice.

Dark wind of his violent death—
Determined, Argus-eyed—
Stirs fiercely now with Freedom's breath.
Take heed, take heed! America!
Step with love, with pride
Into his gigantic stride!

In Memoriam
Dr. Martin Luther King, Jr.
Advocate for his race
Assassinated April 4, 1968

DESOLATE NIGHT

Now is the night of our Gethsemane
When the pernicious enemy
Appears from out of nowhere
To betray again our young and fair.

Crawling with unseen evil
Insidious, almost physical
Is this dark night over America—
Once the hallowed basilica

For the oppressed of every land:
The poor, the refugee, the firebrand
Who sought for himself—*for his sons*—freedom
From want, from martyrdom.

What seed within us breeds this bloody
        dissidence;
What noxious air, this mindless improvidence,
When from one another we are alienated
And compassionate men are assassinated?

For Senator Robert F. Kennedy
Dead from an assassin's bullet,
June 6, 1968

IMMOLATION OF A PRESIDENT

These were the serpents
Sent to destroy his accomplishments:

His inability to find the metaphor
For a long and bloody war.
The wheeler-dealer smear;
The image of a sermoneer.

These were the serpents
Sent to destroy his accomplishments:

The unfulfilled vision
Of becoming the halcyon
To quiet angry, turbulent seas
Of Vietnam doubts, poverty, racial agonies.

These were the serpents
Sent to destroy his accomplishments:

Drop-outs and flowered hippies—
Soiled, unfragrant fraternities.
Senseless violence of dreaded streets.
Old men, and young, plagued with self-deceits.

Pill-takers, dope addicts;
Pornography that poisons and contradicts
The nobleness of the human soul
Found drinking from a dirty bowl.

Once revered America—
Now become without honour, anathema—
Smelled, to the portal of heaven,
Of greed; dead hope, dead men.

Himself agonized, he uttered the word beyond
recall
And set out to cleanse his country's Augean stall.
Then it was that selfless act, that memorable day
Built fair his monument for History to assay.

In tribute to
Lyndon Baines Johnson
President of the United States, 1963-1968

THE GENERAL MUST SLEEP

Under his Library,
Buried in a crypt,
Lies the *bel-esprit*
Of history's famous battle;
A reluctant
Pimpernel
In the face
Of a turbulent world betraying
 his victory's grace.

And—for *all* mankind—Freedom,
Glimpsed at Normandy's beachhead,
Is yet a delirium
In the books stacked
Over his head.

From a half-continent away,
West Point with its reveilles
Arouses memories of its renowned son,
While his country prays—
In sudden appreciation
Of its heritage—

That God may increase
In *his* image
The soldier of peace.

In tribute to
General Dwight D. Eisenhower
President of the United States 1953-1961
Dead March 27, 1969

BETWEEN HAWK AND BUZZARD

He *dared* to snatch from heaven
The fire he gave to her . . .
Reviving her with its warmth.
No longer, then, did she feel the cold

Of exile outside the Eden,
She had hardly had glimpse of.
What he did not, could not know—
Or did, but could not realize—

Was that this bolt of lightning
He stole to reanimate
Her pitifully dazed heart
Mortally struck him with love for her.

Then, king of wide creation,
He gave to her its kinship:
The playfulness of a pup;
Gentle touch of a little lamb . . .

The courage of a lion,
Possessiveness of his mate . . .
Hyena's silly laughter;
And great cats' laziness in the sun . . .

Salty cries of landward gulls;
Elusiveness of an eel . . .
The lust of a surprised goat;
The apprehension of a doe . . .

So that with her—precocious
In a golden, moonbeamed bed
Or covered with a bright, blue sky—
Nothing was wanting in all creation.

Exquisite delight! As close
To heaven as the gusto
Of early morning's cock—
Or ravishment of Apollo gone!

Nothing, nothing was wanting.
All knowledge he gave to her
Save the knowledge
Of his need for her . . .

Thus, the rock he is chained to; and
This need—now that she is gone—
That gnaws at him day by day,
And at night renews his hopes with dreams

Of her—as she was to him, for so long,
So short a time ago.

FOR BACHELORS

The soil grows mouldy and stale
Without inducement, without detail—
And wildest seeds miscarry
Grace and delicate discovery.

EVEN TODAY

Entrenched in a man's home—
His citadel—sex resists intrusion.
Rancid in those who roam—
No parallel—sex assists pollution.

OF ALL SEASONS

Tasting
Winter's ice
On her lips,

He turns up
His collar
Against

The chill
Of her flesh,
Her hands . . .

And rides
Out the storm,
Remembering

Her eyes—warm, wet
Springtides of
Passion.

Remembering her,
Not long before,
Indian-summer

Warm. Alive!
To the magic
Of autumn

In his hands
Close to her face,
Her heart . . .

He steadies
Himself now
At the rail of his belief:

Foreordained
By nature,
Spring follows winter—

And he has,
For his,
A woman of all seasons.

LOVE WAS EVER A RAINBOW

The first savage word
Escaped her love tonight;
And pain—a gallow's bird—
Splintered, like rain, the sunlight

In her eyes still undone
Remembering him—the one
Of the dark wing and scarlet crest—
Plunging, in his quest of her mouth,
Into her breast.

THE SAME THING AS IT WAS TOLD IN A DIFFERENT WORLD

Her nipples are as grapes—
Small, green-eyed
On the vine—

Until Apollo,
        discarding cloudy drapes,
Stretches knowingly from hill
        to clough to hillside;
Then, tipping his golden vessel,
Fills them to bursting with sweet purple wine.

INCOMPATIBILITY

Thirsted by the hot sun in his veins
And maddened by his vision
Of glistening water,
He struggles mightily to obtain it.

Only to find it was a mirage
When, at last,
He bends over
A dry, parched bed.

THE IMPORTANCE OF TOUCH

It is the touch that is ensnarled,
Twisted before it reaches the flesh;
Reluctant, hesitant and gnarled
With whimsy, hidden but ever fresh,

That withholds the hand required by Love's
        poverty—
To soothe the heart and mind;
To assure forgiveness for necessity;
To point the magnetic north of lives entwined.

Hands outstretched—
Though mutual-willed and ringed—
Soft on the arm, the face, afford space . . .
Facility to those hearts that once were winged.

UNEXPECTED HAPPENING

What, then, from me to you, my darling?
Who, of all this world alone,
Fills this hungry starling
With food before unknown.

Could it be
Not just one more happening,
But a willing Odyssey,
Into everlasting Spring?

THE WIFE OF A NIGHTWORKER

Her skin was porcupine
In that hour he drove Braille
On a white-livered, bloodhound line
Without bark or a wagging tail

To guide him this night of fog,
Opaque darkness, and silence
On that lonely road, this lonely time. Nor frog,
Nor bird, nor his prescience

Brought his loved voice out of an ear-pained
Vigil to her. Nor clever manipulation.
Nor self-confidence. Only tears unchained:
To sign with God her utter desolation

Without him.

ALASKAN HERITAGE
(From Cheechako to Sourdough)

This is a story in verse: The yarn
Of a man named John
Who dreamed, as a growing boy,
Of Alaska, of challenge and joy.

He was raised to be unafraid
By a mother, fearless to upbraid
This boy, her son: The guarantee
Between her flesh and immortality.

As he grew, year in, year out,
There was no doubt
His imagination was flexed
By tales of ice-shrouded, North Atlantic
wrecks.

With tricycle, scooter, bicycles,
Friends and Honda motorcycles,
His dreams grew taller than he
While his skills were induced by his curiosity.

Machines, engines, pumps and motors,
Lathes, chains, belting, borers,
Screws, hammers, nails, rope—
To him: A metal, a wood kaleidoscope.

Gear wheels, turnscrews, wrenches, spanners,
Axles, pinions, wheels and sanders,
Pullies, jacks, springs, more rope—
And, to see the stars, his telescope.

At last, a man become, and with blackest hair,
All at once, he was aware
Of a dark and laughing lass;
Of her eyes—his only looking glass.

So, he married. And his family grew:
A boy was born; and then, a girl was due . . .

Now to Alaska's glacier-land
He must go, far from crowds and sunburned sand;
To the land of blizzards, ice floes, boreal light;
Tundra eerie in the aurorean night . . .

And to field upon field of forget-me-not,
Where he could leave his house, his car unlocked;
Where folks refuse to condescend;
And a stranger, at sight, becomes a friend.

Name-droppers there, thoroughly abhored,
Are considered airy bores.
But friendly hands and honest eyes,
Residents warmly rhapsodize.

In this land, rugged and remote,
He hoped to find the antidote
To ruthlessness—for in this, of all states,
Its folklore forever commemorates

Every spirit, free and wild,
And by nature unreconciled
To man's stringency to man
Be he cleric, fisher, or antediluvian.

Now to this, the last frontier,
John would come as a *timberstere*—
To the home of the caribou
And the Sitka black-tailed deer.

In *Denali*, as proletariat
Or plutocrat—it mattered not—he would find
        his habitat
Among Dall sheep, tourists, king crab, whales
        and Asians;
Tlingits, timber, salmon, seals; oil; and bears
        and Russians.

Thus it was to Alaska he came—
A Cheechako who pinned his star to wife and crew,
        to tame
A towering forest: cutting, rafting, tugging timber—
Lumber for homes and schools
        and for the international builder.

Mightily does his labor increase.
With each log, he foresees the ships, the factories
His joy, his strength produces . . .
Thus, with care, he reseeds the precious spruces.

Proudly then in this, her hundredth year,
Alaska—pleased with this hardy,
this undaunted pioneer—
In '67, with twin sons doubled his yield
And dubbed the Cheechako a true *Sourdough*
indeed!

A tale—*for them to remember*—
Dedicated to the author's
Four Alaskan godchildren:
John S. Bond, Jr.; his sister, Melody;
And their twin brothers, David and Bruce.

"IF I HAD AT LEAST ENRICHED THE EARTH . . ."

She, herself, herself betagged.
Precipitantly was she snagged
By unknown, unwanted reeds presaging
The heedless thievery of aging.

Prostrated by the Plunderer,
Anxious sex is not forever.
And now, the slant of wind
Betrays the years—barren, undisciplined.

*"LET HIM HAVE DOMINION"**

Eagle cleaves the sky
And pinions the moon
With his talons!

Earthlings! Have confidence
To become, to each, full of grace,
Beauteous!

Apollo, lifting up your hearts
With an everlasting imperiality
Vouchsafed in God's primeval opinion,

Wings hope to Man—courageous, *tremulous*—
To scatter his seed on distant stars;
To achieve, at last, his dream of immortality.

To celebrate Neil Armstrong
The first man on the moon
July 20, 1969

*Genesis 1:26

MAN! KNOW WHAT I MEAN, MAN?

It is a game
Of piquet
Hippies play

With anything—Amen!—
Below Card
7

(Its design, Love's)
        Shunned—
                Jettisoned!

By their own decree
        To keep them
                Free

Of disenthrallment—
A comedy
Of forestallment . . .

The card below seven,
Now and then,
Turning up

When least expected
In the game—
Arrow-headed

Toward hearts
Once grassed;
Now embarrassed

To acknowledge at last—
Oh, Heart! What are your measurements?—
An experience forecast, yea man!
        even *understood* by parents!

MOTHER-EARTH

Still there is a beauty sensed
Beneath the opacity of her dead dream—
Which icily hides her soul incensed
With fratricide, and all her sons demeaned.

A POET CONTEMPLATES A REJECTION SLIP

Bob White! Bob White! Bob White!
With such a small note to sing,
Evening rings with your insistence.

Bob White! Bob White! Bob White!
Hear me! Look at me! Hear me!
O, happy, inborn impudence!

The while a huge, golden light
Opens its casement in the sky
And mutes hearts with quiet eloquence.

ROBERT MOSES

Immovable
Sparkling granite,
This face of quartz
Shines now for all
The *World* to see:
More lustrous than
His *Fair*.

Hornblendic rage
At blind small men
Revealed in his
Feldsparian
Nature a deep
Craggy cleavage
Spewing

Volcanic stones
On those who would
Obstruct dreams—not
Even guessing
The right-angled
Road leading to
His heart

That igneous
Rock which, flame-touched
Under mica
Laminae, changed
Hot city streets
Into lazy sand
Beside

Light-hearted waves;
And a
Red-bricked, green-tipped
Water Tower—
Symbol of joy—
Into an
Ocean obelisk.

SLEEP WELL

The sun is ambushed
And netted is his light.
Then softly, from afar,
Comes God's goodnight
Through a bramble-bush of stars.

UNHINGED IN OUR TIME

More! More! O God! dear Love,
Of Christmas with its shining light . . .
Its crèche where coos a mourning dove—
The messenger of peace: the tender Bethlehemite.

More! More! O God! of pleasure-trips,
Of coffee in bed and packages bright,
Boots, paintings, a bowl, a book; of friendships
Warm to the hand, and watertight.

For tomorrow . . .

Tomorrow resumes the argumentation
That stultifies the masses . . .
The battle, the strife, the assassination
That shocks the bewildered classes.

Ah! Bells of Notre Dame!
Wherefore, wherein your shame?

DEATH COMES WITH SOFT LAUGHTER

Less than twice
A baker's dozen
Were his years
Hardly yet aspen-

Leafed with tears.
Family, altar,
Books man-shaped
His mind, his laughter.

Oh! Happy,
Tortured, sparkling years—
Ice-fringed with
Earnest, humble fears—

Their prize: White
Jacket'd stethescope
Eavesdropping
Pain with healing hope.

Pitiful,
Pitiful twenty-
Four deserves
Tears; and such pity,

In substance,
As does his father's
Recalling
With sharpened focus

His own young
Love—eager, hungried
For this son,
Stiff now with lifeless seed.

For a young intern-friend
Killed by a hit-and-run driver
as he was saying goodnight to
his friends in front of his
hospital.

AN IRISH MOTHER

"Mary, come Home,"
Said God, months and months ago.
But Mary—*didn't she once have red and shining hair?*—
Was not about to leave; but coaxed Him in her irresistible way
To let her stay a while to see
And smile once more upon,
Or—*who minds pain?*—to inquire for
By name, those near and not too far, her own:

The sixty-five human beings
To whom she was Mother
And Grand-
And great-Gran'Ma.
All of them—*didn't she teach them?*—destined too for heaven.

Moreover, she wanted time
For remembering—*would she ever forget?*—
How his hand, tentative with wonder,
Throbbed to each new pulse
His love had gifted her womb

The while, with the other
He tilted her head until her soft, blue eyes—
Irish they were!—met male eyes
That laughed with pride
As he reminded her:

It was he, William Barry Leitch—
He couldn't have been more Irish if he'd
been born in Ireland!—
Who was the progenitor
Of this great, new family . . .

The family that produced
A butcher; a baker—*who was that?*—
A candlestick maker—*and that?*—
And one who followed the sea;

Teachers, writers, administrators,
Entrepreneurs, thoughtful educators
And oh! the splendid one—*she'd be seeing*
him soon—
Who might have become the scientist.

But nothing accomplished
By this charmed and charming darlin'
Meant so much to her—
Or truly to the world!—

As the exceedingly singular
And most awesome fact
Dear, blessed God, remember?
That she was, besides,

The mother of a priest.

Remembering
Mary J. Leitch
August 25, 1967

THE JEWELED CROWN

The fire of the flesh long since
Had ceased to warm his bones.
Only the knowledge that she was there
Beside him

Gave him the enduring courage
His frail frame denied him.
She was a tower bearing twin lamps
To guide him—

Lamps for him not only, but for all
Who stood within their beam.
She was the lighter of the darkness
In the heart,

Who roused sleeping aspirations
With the flash of her eyes;
A charm to inert talent fresh or
Old from God.

Well may the old man stumble and
Cry out in the darkness,
Now that the light of his morning star's
Extinguished.

Well may he sob; well may he sob—
Not yet aware
Of the jeweled crown she left atop his
Anguished head.

In memory of my friend,
Susan Rose Albin

A PREREVOLUTIONARY TEACHER

Since 1921
I have saluted her,
Every one
Of my thoughts a debtor

To the teacher vexed
At the wandering decimal
Or words in exile, out of context;
The classical disciplinarian
Undisturbed, unperplexed
By rebellion—not then expressed—
        against the analytical grammarian.

Oh the years!—fifty-four in number—
When as teacher, friend academical,
Her countenance would bestir
The days to smile or sag, not one to another
        identical.

So too today as, bursting her golden chrysalis,
She flies unfettered toward the sun:
Caroline Pullis
(The headline reads) *is dead at 91.*

For my eighth grade teacher
April 21, 1969

LOVE IS INSCRUTABLE

He is culpable
To the one he found impeccable;
Deplorable
To the one he found delectable.

Cock-and-bull
To the one he found commendable;
Unredeemable
To the one he thought amenable.

He is incomprehensible
To the one he found so sensible;
Ostensible
To the one he thought perceptible.

He finds it incredible
That two such as they can be so inflexible.
But *she* knows, being woman and infallible,
That their love is infrangible . . . ineffable.

WHAT IS THE NAME OF PAIN?

A body rent by child at birth?
Onslaught of death's impartial thirst?

A woman can forget, unprayed,
The terrifying price she paid

To bring a child to cry, to life—
The race made certain, secured by mother-wife.

Souls who drop their earthly clothes
Are free, at last, in God's repose.

And a fair facsimile of love
Can stir again the mourning-dove . . .

Is this then the name of pain?

Imprisoned spirit, captive mind
Too long apart from truth, from kind?

Yet friends, a book, the wassail-bowl
Resuscitate the mind, the soul.

But who relieves the pained abyss
Engulfing little children, this

To see: Their father dead and odd—
And *told* this is an act of God?

THE YOUNG SPEEDER

At Atropos' swift command
The Keeper of the Spindle
Cut the thread of his young life
And, with her conniving sisters,

Broods now over this male child
Who fearlessly measured
His archangel's shining sword
With a circumventive world.

His latent masculine strength
Might have fathered a man's work—
His destiny was to cast
Into hell with one wild stroke

The dark spirits who prowl
The night of nuclear exile
Thwarting immature desires,
Unhorsing fugitive dreams.

What does innocent seventeen know
Of the ultimate act with which
The Prince of Frustration
Nullifies life?

What does seventeen know of God?
What does he know
Save that his heart is unhinged
In our time?

And what—
In our time—
Would satisfy him
Except that he be still in His Hand?

SOUNDS HEARD WITH EARLY MORNING COFFEE

A sounding string of tiny matched pearls
Are the soft, vibrating notes
Of the robins, fresh to spring
As adolescent girls.

School bullies, with noisy stratagem,
Are the bluejays in their mischief—
Doers to others of those things
They would not have done to them.

The kiss-and-tell type
Is heard in the cock's exultant boasting;
While nearby crows, dressed in widow's clothes,
Harshly caw and gripe.

An aging citizen he bemocks—
This lonely bird whose sharp, one-note squeak
Overcomes the neighborhood: A rusty pulley
With its clotheslines filling up with socks.,

Now comes the sound
That cups a smile in our early morning coffee
Spreading in happy rings as we listen,
Spellbound,

To a brilliant red cardinal
        and his children's mother,
Joyful communicators—
In love, in friendship—
Singing their hearts out to one another.

THE *SANTA MARIA*, THE *NIÑA* AND THE *PINTA*

August 3, 1492
Spain

The port of Palos was wrapped in torch-lit
darkness—
The morning sun yet half an hour
Below the far horizon—when all
The sails unfurled their wings above Columbus.

EL SALVADOR
(An Accident of Discovery)
October 7, 1492

The southwest passage of birds—
All this long night—
Led Colón to change his course.
Guanahani . . .
        Strange island . . .
                New World!

MISTAKEN IDENTITY
October 12, 1492

A being descended from heaven!
The awed, fearful natives thought him . . .
Equally mistaken,
Columbus called them *Indian.*

PASCULA FLORIDA

Eastertime, 1513

Ponce de León

Vain was the Spaniard's search for springtime.
Youth is this land—is the rain which
Falls on the verdant peninsula named for
Easter—first feast of the Church for all time.

MISSISSIPPI RIVER

Sighted May 21, 1541,
by Hernando de Soto;
His grave, May 21, 1542

He left behind to guard his fleet
A hundred men off Florida's coast;
Then marched toward western plains
With hosts of men and horses bold,
Disarming tomahawks en route.

No tribe, no Indian chief, but
A fever stalled de Soto's heart.
In grief, and fear of scalping knife,
One year to the very day
They hailed the Mississippi's banks,

His soldiers slipped their captain—
Mute and cold in a winding sheet—
To the Father of the Waters.

WATERIE LABYRINTH*

By his own words—now beyond recall—
It was *his*: The mighty task to cleanse
Our souls, our Augean stall,
Amid bloody and raucous dissents.

Drums of honor beat incessantly
In solemn phrase, deliberate gaze
As he led us from Gethsemane
Secreting, the while, his dark malaise.

There is something, now, he leaves
Imperfect in the state,
Apprehended since the eaves-
Dropping at Watergate,

Which imports to the nation
Great danger, greater fear
For our destination,
And truth turned insincere.

No! No! No! Not these hypocrisies
In the white, most sacred citadel—
Trusted fortress of democracy's
Freedoms, America's sentinel.

An eyeless monster, a foul madness
With piercing sight stalks, incarnadine,
Marring ideals, our comeliness,
Murdering the spirit of children.

Still . . .

For America's honor, we yearn
That he may for truth be purified;
Shriven, in his personal return
Most necessary now; required.

Based on the Legend of Hercules;
Shakespeare's *King Lear*, Act IV, sc. iii
(paraphrased).

*Milton: *Paradise Lost*, Book II.

CAN THE COCOON HOLD A BUTTERFLY FOREVER?

Two pools of rippling blue,
Stirred by stones of gold
Tossed gleefully by the sun,
Were passage to his soul.

Title to his inheritance,
A crown of brilliant red;
And to his Father's House
The sweet fragrance of a little child.

His spirit—a diamond
Cut by God Himself—
Shed its pure fire
In the harmony

Of his manners—
In meticulous dress;
The way words lay in his eyes;
The way a smile graced his face . . .

Revealed its shimmering light
Dancing tremulously in his play
While reaching for a leaf;
Or for love

So happily received.
So doubly, triply, infinitely given
By those who, with Heaven,
Heard the beating of the Wings

He did not hear.

Or perhaps he *did?*

For by what divine intuition
Did he shy away
From boys' rough play—
Accepting little girls

For gentler childhood joys,
If not to hold taut for a moment longer
The string on God's finger which was wound
Around his little heart?

In memory of my grandnephew
Steven Couch
December 6, 1965 - July 13, 1972

FROM THIS TIME ON

I shall tarry
With this shining memory.
But more—
And evermore—

I shall recall
Friendship's windfall over the years:
Yours and mine,
By accident or design.

Nor shall I forget
The debt
Owed each of you:
For there were *entre nous*

Our *Good Morning! Good Night!*
May your holidays be bright!
Hi, Cherubs! Be good!
(And, to the boss)
I'm glad you understood . . .

Beyond that,

I thank you
For your eyes shined with dew
Over your wedding albums;
For the triumphant look of your bridegrooms.

I thank you
For the strength of working fathers;
The stamina of working mothers.
For their sacrifice, their fortitude,
Their dreams for their broods . . .

To every new grandchild
Who beguiled
Its grandmother (and the office force),
My memory will have recourse.

To my young co-workers, a grace-cup
For being fed up
With sham and dishonesty.
We spoke . . . *I* am *your* legatee.

All of you joyed me with your happiness;
Pained me when you were comfortless.
No matter: Your names,
In prayer, were flames.

To the Commission
Entrusted so long with my ambition,
I say: You were my home
Away from home.

You were my bread;
The arrow-head
That delivered me
From my enemy.

But more—
And forevermore—

I am mindful,
And grateful,
That—from this time on—
You also provide the anchorage
To steady the ship of this, my greatest age.

Upon my Retirement from
the Long Island State Park
and Recreation Commission

October 3, 1974

ENVIRONMENT FOR RETIREMENT

Pulsing drums of unmuffled traffic,
Sudden shouts from a school nearby,
Ear-splitting, persistent, heart-breaking sirens
By day, and by night, assail this bailiwick.

My proud flags are officially furled.
But these harsh, insistent sounds alone
Forbid shutting out the constant busyness
Of the world outside my world.

I am *alive!* Alive to

My *Champs-Elysées*—broad avenue
Spreading below my study window;
The gulls flying over it, flying southward—
Seaward—on a day about to clear and shine.

My black, glistening *roof-tops* of *Paris*
Yawning, stretching to the rising sun,
Whose light, creeping across my breakfast table,
Suddenly bursts asunder the armistice of the night

I am *alive!* Alive to

The eyeless beauty of gnarled trees across
the court;
Orange berries plucked by winged hunger
From the mountain ash below my balcony—
Cedar-hugged for the private sport of cats.

Through my living room window

Not one nor another a replica:
Flamed sunsets, enormous purple skies,
Clouds, moons, golden stars—the *whole*
panorama
Of heaven!—unrolling.

My rooms fill with, are attuned to

Sounds of New Orleans; Beethoven.
Dorothy Stickney evoking
The spirit of Edna St. Vincent Millay.
And sherry flows.

I am *alive!* Alive to

Walls hung with paintings dearly treasured;
Loved ones fixed forever in their frames;
Book-burdened shelves, the grey desk
in my study
Where, sans pretense, my confidence is assured.

Everything that inspires is here,
Save the one thing that makes a heart sing:
A human being who laughs, and loves,
        and talks—
A human being who breathes, and moves,
        and hears.

I am alive. *Half* . . .

CONCEPTION

Exalted is the night, yet vague,
That holds Creation's mystery
When a man, with sluice-gate raised,
Releases into the fragrant valley
Of his domain

Mighty waters laden with his seed
In extravagant excess:
An intrepid army of sperm,
Three hundred million strong, who—
While trailing providential stores—
Use their tails as oars
In blind pursuit of their holy grail:
A single, almost invisible egg.

At last, one sperm—the strongest,
Most tenacious of the pack,
O Bold Adventurer!—
Dashes headlong into a darkened cave
And, without raising his cap,
Claims his victory, yet is himself
Surprised, entrapped, even as
He stamps his blazon on his prize.

Ever after—O Adamite Pride!—
Man's self-esteem exceeds the gods':
He is the creator of life! he boasts,
Instead of being the more modest co-maker.

For there'd be no life without
The egg; nor, the woman knows,
Without the sperm; nor, God knows,
Without the lady's own blazon—
Made, from all Eternity,
Equal to the invading host's.

WHAT IS IN A NAME?

Shakespeare said a rose
Would smell as sweet
By any other name.

But Gertrude Stein insisted
A rose is a rose
Is a rose is a rose.

Names relay the image,
The identity of dragonflies
And men,

As any rock group,
Or any boy called Percy,
Knows.

Doubly entrapping are these,
Raising their proud heads
Or bowing them:

John and Henry,
Catherine and Elizabeth—
Royal names

Borne, over and over again,
By kings and queens . . . but before them,
by the saints.

Some names are scarcely separable
In recognizing good
And evil.

Such is the name of Love—
The badge of Man's highest emotion—
Which today,

As in days gone by,
Oft-times becomes a cameo camouflaging
His blackest agony.

LAURRAINE GOREAU

O Poet! Bravissimo! *Bravissimo!*
No adversity—nor yet Mahalia's dizzying
  undertow—
Stopped you from doing the work
God ordained for you, Laurraine Goreau;

Neither did the confined frustration,
Nor the secret suffering that halts
Ordinary mortals in their aimless tracks.
O inspiring, inspired Inspiration!

Out of your pain
Came one of your loveliest songs
About remembered rain
You said direct to God belongs.

With reverential awe,
You felt it *indoors*—
The very same rain that fell
On Adam's head, then from his bearded jaw;

The very same water God created
To fill up the rivers, the lakes, and the seas
From which His Hand scoops it back, up
  to heaven,
To spill it—over and over—again.

This is the same Hand you grasped yesterday
    morning,
When He reached out to you, nor were you
    surprised
To feel It as light as morning dew,
As soft as summer rain;

As tender as every living thing
On earth
In which you had recognized
God's wondrous disguise.

Farewell, dear Poet! for just a while.
Farewell, dear *Sister*—so strong
In your ancient Faith, it glowed
With renascent grace in your amazing face.

Farewell, Laurraine Goreau!
Farewell, O blissful Smile!
As you go to the Altar of God
Bearing your Gift in your hands . . .

And the *Christus* in your heart.

September 12, 1985

A MEETING BETWEEN OLD FRIENDS*

Little did he know—
When he exchanged two oranges
For the other-world look in Laurraine's eyes—
That in less than five years
He'd be seeing her again.

While she was still in her body,
He saw her rise *angel-like*.
And now pure spirit,
Indeed an angel rises to greet him . . .
Only—considering his years—
More like a tear in that place
Where no one cries, nor for unwritten poems
Bulging his pockets like oranges.

Now—become both Virgil
And Beatrice to him
In that genderless heaven—
She tells him of the certainty
She discovered there . . .

That the home he built
For homeless poets
Was--and will ever be—
Their shelter not only,
But also their foretaste

Of the spiritual joys
Given in fullness forever
To poets face to face—but worthily—
With their Creator whose voice
They echoed on earth.

Like everyone who knew him,
She had known the quality of his friendship—
Had he not come to the Dominican Home
To taste her words with her?
To encourage her?
Had he not driven her regularly
Across town to the poets' house
For fellowship with spirits
Kindred to her own?

Had he any idea
How much he had relieved
Her pain?

For such kindness
A soul is promised heaven . . .

And for this—
Describing for the blind
Visions they cannot see,
Expressing for the tongue-tied
Longings pressing their sides.

Even now he had said to her,
I brought you something from home.

* * * * *

Later on—
Oh, how the Wind blew!—
Carefully, with delicacy,
They bit into two red-gold oranges
Laurraine Goreau found
In Ed Vickers' pocket.

In memory of
Edward Davin Vickers
Founding President
Georgia State Poetry Society

*Inspired by
Two Oranges for Laurraine
by Edward Davin Vickers

IN A ROSE GARDEN

Beauty—resplendent
In a bridal gown;
Regal, confident
Of today's bright crown—

Pauses, unplanned,
Beside a single flower—
Walled, unscanned—
In a rose-drenched bower.

Cool, wet petals glistening
While the love light in her eyes—
Virginal, listening—
Intensifies.

Off guard now are her leafy Hesperides.
Their dark-skinned shadows, restless,
Designed anew by the traitor-breeze—
Accomplice, at once, in Apollo's gold caress.

Penelope smiles . . .
An act of grace, long since spiriting
        her father's hands,
Blessedly unafraid of unknown trials
The fates may send to test her nuptial-bands.

INTRUSION

Sleep slips away. Will not be caught
Tonight. Who can dream with moonlight
Hanging a white shade, *cross-beamed*
With somber thought, on my bedroom door?

While dazzling light excites
The hound to bay hoarsely at the fox,
He imagines—monomaniac!—
Fleeing through the wood that interlocks
Red streakéd clay.

The bass of frogs
Sings with the high strings of insects;
Nature's non-soothing, nocturnal dialogue
Orchestrated beneath the blinding
Spotlight in the sky.

SEVEN NEW MOONS FOR URANUS

O dreadful catastrophe!
Seven moons—doomed satellites
Trailing white-hot debris—
Plunged—before our very eyes!—
Down, down, down the skies

Into a restless sea,
Whose surging foam hauled
Ashes from charred craters
Unrecognizable to all
But Rome (long acquainted with the holy)

And Aphrodite—hymned Venus
Veined as a rose—who first arose
From the sea, out of the foam
That swirled about the limbs
Of Uranus.

Today, Love appears again,
But red-eyed and in tears,
Stirring a hallowed passion in men
Who watched her touch such sorrow
And such fears

In hearts shocked by the Seven's
Encounter with Gaea's ancient fury
Against Uranus, who—
This time, victorious!—
Swoops up the Astro-moons

For the *Menorah*
In his heavenly Temple—
To shine *forever*
By the light of the joyful aspirations
Of seven glorious creations.

In memory of the
Seven American Astronauts,
including teacher Christa McAuliffe,
who perished with their
space-shuttle CHALLENGER,
74 seconds after lift-off,
January 28, 1986

ROY WILKINS AT HYDE PARK

Roy Wilkins is dead . . .
And I remember
The barren-spirited day
When I first met him—the day

Eleanor was laid to rest
In the rose garden
Beside Franklin, the squire
Of Hyde Park,
The betrayer of her heart.

Under a massive leafless tree,
I stood at the curb,
Sorely pressed by the crowd
Surging to see the dead
Who would be passing by.

She came at last
With a single flashing light
And silently passed us
With a string of limousines
Following her through the iron gate
To her wet and gaping grave.

But not before President Kennedy,
Turning his head from side to side,
Smiled and waved to the people
Beside themselves with cheers,
Nor guessing the shocked tears
Lying in wait for them
In just the year ahead.

And there were Eisenhower
And Truman,
Any many others I recall;
But these, with their ladies,
Towered over all.

Nor did I foresee
That this was the day
I was to meet Roy Wilkins
Later, in a little shop
On the way out of town
Where my friend and I stopped
For a cup of tea.

He was sitting at the counter,
Having coffee and danish,
With his beautiful wife.
I recognized him
From pictures I'd seen
In the *Times*.

And I wondered
Why he chose to sit at a counter
Up North; and seven years after Rosa.

GOLDA MEIR
1898—1978

Good and faithful was this servant—
Herself one of the wandering Jews—
Who, years before their *bête noire*
Consumed their hallowed millions,

Dreamed of the return to Jerusalem
Of those set adrift by Romans,
Of those in homeless misery roaming
Since the fated year of A.D. Seventy.

In 1921 and for seven years—
The seeding-time of Israel—
This passionate lover of Zion
Wore boots at the Merẖavya kibbutz.

So was lit the *Shammash*—the servant candle—
That kindled—one by one—the days
Of her creation to and beyond
The year 1948,
When Israel became a nation.

Ah yes, Golda Meir!—
Builder of houses, of roads;
Organizer of labor;

Minister to foreign needs;
Shepherd of immigrants;
Beggar of funds;
Beggar, above all, of peace
With secure borders.
Then, in your old age,
Prime Minister of the State!—

Ah yes!
Brightly does your *Menorah* shine
In Israel, where your Israelis
Celebrate Hanukka freely
And remember your gifts to them.

But peace eludes them still
And the dawn is shrill across the land
Causing anguished hearts,
While you are safe with your Fathers
And their God.

Oh, Golda Meir!
You must know *something* there
That is unknown here—

If you do, dear Mother of Israel,
Please calm your children's fears?

For Golda Meir, a founder of Israel

IRAN, O NEGLIGENT MOTHER!

Their laughter became gas,
Deprived even of its last gasp,
When these shooting stars
Shot to earth . . .

Little ones blown out of the sky,
Fallen from their mothers
Who had no arms to hold them,
Fallen into the lap of the sea,
Into his arms.

There his startled waves
Made a gurgling sound
As they broke apart
To stroke them all around.
They had been playmates,
Affectionate. Articulate
In their own way.

The sea god himself recalled
How all the children laughed
—was it only the day before?—
When he sent his own
To play tag with them
On his Crescent shores
At Persia's Bander Abbas.

Oh, how they squealed!
How they teased one another
—just yesterday!—
Running back and forth
To and fro in and out of the sea,
Their screeching secret—
To touch toes,
Then swift as undertows,
Run the other way,
Away from one another.

* * * * *

Why do they lie so still?
They're much too quiet
For little boys and girls . . .
Strangely silent.
Unnatural.

Who could believe?
The sea king bent over
For a closer look—

And heaved.

July 3, 1988

A LIGHT GOES OUT IN EGYPT

Oh! Cry, O Heart!
Oh! Mourn, O World!
Sadat, the Man of Peace,
Is ripped to death
In Egypt.

His crime?
He embraced the Jews,
And Christians too.

And for this
He fell from grace;
And for this
He was destroyed.

And for this
His brother Muslims
Dance overtime
With joy.

Oh! Cry, O Heart!
For that noble corpse.

Oh! Mourn, O World!
For warped minds
Blind to his vision;

For ears deaf to what
Sadat could hear,
The dead crying:

Get on with living!
For Allah is not
The God of the dead,
But of the living!

Let tears fall
For the light blacked out
In Egypt,
Whose great house
Suffers a plague
More horrible, now,
Than all the plagues
Under Pharaoh.

Cry! Cry! O Heart!
Mourn! Mourn! O World!
Whither the middle East?
Whither Peace?
Whither the world? . . .
Since he no longer speaks.

For Anwar Sadat,
President of Egypt,
Assassinated October 6, 1981

THE NUCLEAR BEASTS

Never! Never will fire-snorting beasts
Be content to be tethered in their stalls.
Made to rampage and ravish the world,
Even now they stomp and strain for release.

Two men alone—of all the men on earth—
Will decide fate if they free these furies
Whose lethal genes are passed on, *multiplied*
A thousand-fold with each generation's birth.

Rise up, peoples of the Earth! Government
Must not be allowed to loose these mad beasts
And their offspring, who will destroy you
With firey breath or their black excrement.

So soon and so horribly must you die?
Who can survive cindered flesh and bones?
Escapees with no legs? No arms? No sight
In liquefied eyes? They will *cry* to die!

Anno Domini—The year of the Lord—
Has become *Anno Diaboli:*
The year of the Devil, desperate
For the souls of men. Save! Save us, O Lord!

Send Your Spirit to the two, in West
and East,
Who would tarnish the silver of Your stars;
Would blacken Your earth and sky
with clouds
Mushrooming from the red-eyed beasts.

O Day of Wrath! There is no place to hide.
Babies torn from the wombs of dead women,
Children consumed by the flame-mouthed
beasts,
And millions would not know how they
had died.

Sad, sorry world, so beautiful and blue!
Even the Devil feels sorry for you
And will burn you quickly to crisp,
And innocent children—your lambs—
and their ewe.

So the Earth and its every living soul
Can perish, Is *that* what you want, O Man?
For you and yours? For your children? For Earth
To disappear into a black, black hole?

1982

THE TOAD, REMEMBERING, HIDES HIS HEAD

For five hundred to two thousand millennia
(Plus or minus a few years), since the progenitors
Of the human race appeared (and quickly became
    anathema
To Him), God's true nature remained hidden,
    secular,
Overcast by the image of a God of vengeance
    and jealousy
Until Time was split by the Child.
So, too, for all these millennia,
The true nature of Woman remained hidden—
Distorted by some devilish mania—
Ever since Man, willfully ignoring his own
    imperfection,
Burdened Woman with his original defection.
Chattel she became, often kitchen midden,
Coping at once with his strength and his
    concupiscence.
Whether crowned with a golden diadem or clothed
In rags, in self-defense,
She chose subterfuge as her refuge until herself
    she loathed.

No more! No more! Her spirit—tumbling and
shrill-voiced
In the weightlessness of her own daring
To recover her pristine freedom of choice—
This day rose up in fierce anger against the
ensnaring
Of her soul and body, of her very mind.

Take heed, O Man! She rides higher and higher
now,
Stretching her intellect to the heavens. Would
you grind
To dust the stars she sights from the prow
Of her ship as she seeks
Her own salvation for this world and for the next?
Her launching rocket, the ship's velocity,
Is God Himself.

If sweat and tears must flow down her cheeks,
Let them. She is entitled to her own pain,
unperplexed.
No matter which course God sets for her—
careerist,
Homemaker, mother, or simply lover—*life*,
not death,
Is her noble desire for her ordinary gifts
And for those extraordinary, animated now
by freedom's quickening breath.

How strange of Man, how odd!
To think himself the sole recipient of talent—
Talent he knows God
Will take away if not well spent.
Yet he will deny that granted another
And say to her very face:
You are but housewife and mother,
Made only for my demon and my embrace.

His mouth deprived her of her genius;
Swallowed it up in the estuary of his arms—
All trace gone in the tide of history as if God
did never kiss
Her brow, did never give her aught but charms.
Man eroded Woman's gifts like sand
from a beach.

Still he has the audacity
In the marketplace and in the pulpit, to preach
With elaborate and devious perversity:

Your brain is inferior to mine! Remain
In your place! You are inane, and now insane!
You are weak. I am strong! So God did ordain.
I was created in His image. I am lord
of this domain!

But the spirit (the Holy Spirit)
Blows through Woman and she replies:

God's truth will prevail now, and after
You've done with your lies.
How presumptious of you, O Man!—ha! the dinosaur
Was surprised once—to deny freedom to any human
to scar!
To regard Woman inferior!
It was your hand that aborted her gifts (the Auditor
Is God!) You denied them life.
All things in this world—love too—
Are promised enrichment through this strife.
So you are promised, except this myth you still pursue.
Or must I—Woman—be forced, at last, to own
That you were not made in the image of God,
That you made God in your own?

WHIPS AND CHAINS

Ah, foolish, fettered women
Whose men whip
Their minds to unreality

And chain
Their abused bodies
To a questionable lease,

When will you be free?

O EARTH!
WHEN WILL YOUR TENT BE IN PEACE?

I want to write a brave poem
To celebrate this Christmas '79.
To bring the kiss of God to you
To allay your trembling fears.

I want to write a saving poem
Filled with shining stars
To be the acolytes of your heart
To light your coming years.

I want to give to you
A cheerful poem!
A geranium
To set upon your windowsill.

Alas! The night has fallen
And Man is chilled to the bone.
The Star of Bethlehem, grown dim,
No longer guides him Home.

In darkness do I see tonight
Reluctant havens given fleeing brothers
Who survived the savage seas—
But none at all to Mary.

I see Ireland.
Iran. The IRA.
And single-minded guerillas everywhere.
Afghanistan. Cambodia.
Argentina and Vietnam.
China. The Soviet Union.
Cuba. And the U.S.A.

Where will they be
At the end of the century?
Will the enslaved be free?
The free, enslaved?

What delirium will befall
Our planet Earth by then?
What, if any, Runnymede
For us who once were free?

THIS WAY!

This way!—to no less than St. George himself!—
Shouted the boy in boisterous play
As he roared down a hill
To slay "dragons" on a half-mooned shore.

This way, my son, Sara adjured
The child to the manor born,
Is how a gentleman is discovered:
Be caring, always, of the poor.

Franklin! This way! cried Eleanor
To her stricken husband one fateful day:
Up! Up on your feet even in braces,
Or you surely die!

This way! A President told a nation
He found freezing, selling apples
In the streets, stamping numbed feet,
Warming cold hands over ashcan fires:

> *The only thing we have to fear*
> *Is fear itself!*

Suddenly, out of a surprised sky,
Infamous bombs rained from the blue,
Destroying his proud ships,
Entombing forever their agonized crews.

Dismayed by the perfidious trick,
This man of peace
Dared to command, as chief: *This way!*
Then his rockets glared red over the Pacific

And—four days later—
Across the Atlantic,
Where Italy and the bully of Europe
Threatened to bludgeon a crippled nation.

This way! Roosevelt cried out to St. George,
Whose banners were already aflame.
Joining lances and helped
By yeomen subterranean and brave,

They slashed through the Mediterranean boot.
And from the sundered shores of France
Enroute to the dragon's lair,
Freed Europe from its gallows tree.

Now with victory scenting the very air,
But with its triumphant flags not yet unfurled,
This way! said God to the President,
And quietly the man went Home.

A swell of grief engulfed his nation
And the world. And concentration camps,
Where—so close to freedom—all hurled
themselves
Against their blackened walls and wept

For this man forever blessed
For words still lingering on his lips:
Freedom to speak and seek a God of one's own.
Freedom from want, freedom from fear.

And for his alarm:
Abate hate! Cast off excessive arms!
Every nation has the right to peace,
To live without fear.

But today, not forty years
Since his great soul was heaven-borne,
A handful of men, power-crazed,
Decide who lives or dies. And no one
cries . . .

Half the world dare not speak!
Half the world is denied its God.
Whole populations die of hunger
And everywhere fear haunts every single soul.

This way! Roosevelt calls,
Even now, from Eternity,
To a frightened, supine world:
Get up on your feet! Live!

Care for your innocents—
Your poor, your sick,
Your elderly and your young.
Your ignorant.

Protect all creatures and
Your planet! Remember,
It is your only home
Away from Home.

Be jealous of your liberty!

Be watchful of your government.
As I said before, it is better
That charity—not icy indifference—
Cover its occasional sin.

Destroy excess arms
That tempt nations to agression.
But keep your defenses up!
Above all,

HOLD FAST TO YOUR HONOR!

Then you will know,
My friends:
The only thing you have to fear
Is fear itself!

To celebrate
Franklin D. Roosevelt,
32nd President of the United States
and world leader.

BUT ONE REASON FOR WRITING POEMS FOR THE DEAD

There is much more due
To one who dies
Than Death's *in transitu*
Closing of the eyes.

As silence falls
And words remain unsaid,
What trumpet calls the world
To the unspoken dead

Save a poet's heralded lines?

There read the preface
To the book of their seasons.
There sing the *Preface*
That signs the sacred canons

Of the graved and radiant dead,
Whose living caresses
Stamped on generations to come
The golden signet of talent,

Or bravely spun
The thread of discontent
That gave rise to a rebel-son
Or a like-minded daughter.

Ah, yes!

There is much more due
To one who dies
Than Death's *in transitu*
Closing of the eyes.

A CANTERBURY BELL

(Written in the meter and the rhyme of Chaucer's *Prologue*)

When that April with mischief afoot
Played fool with the aspiring root
Blanketing with snow its frail flower
That had been newly born within the hour;
E'en as the Nor'easter, with its breath
So harsh, suddenly rose with threat of death
Causing swirling snowflakes the sun
To hide, small fur home to run,
No small bird to sound, no melody
Except hawk of the gull fleeing the sea,
Then glorious South's mysterious image
In my mind enticed me on a pilgrimage.
I left friends and kin in Babylon
For Georgia's unknown Carrollton,
Whose speech I'd find I could not
comprehend
While my own, I'd fear, strange ears might
offend,
For Northerners and Southerners do speak
In accents odd which others judge unique.
Braving this, and this out-of-season day,
I climbed into my Olds and drove away
Until I crossed the Verrazona Bridge

Where I surprised Geoffrey Chaucer's
pilgrimage
And thrilled to join such lively company—
Pilgrims all—enroute to Canterbury,
The Martyr there to honor; to recall
The saint's scandalous murder that shocked all
Of England and the Continent wide
That twelfth-century revolting Christmas-tide
When Henry's stealthiest knights did wrest
Breath from Becket's body, his soul blest
Forevermore. So ever and anon,
Pilgrims travel to the altar whereon
His blood was shed and eternalized;
Yet not then, nor today, has been apprised
The will in Man to share this world with grace;
T'allow nations and men their private space.
Reading my thoughts, the Knight smiled,
but a frown
From the Merchant did grind me way down
As we rode through polluted Jersey
On and on, and through Washington, D.C.
Where, curious, I learned the Physician
Relied on the stars, and that discipline
Was often lacking in the Church's man.
Who risked both himself and everyman.

Prototype of *it's got to be me*—
The Bath Wife—joined us in ole Virginny:
Five husbands she boasts plus, when younger,
More lovers to feed her gap-toothed hunger.
She was conspicuous in old-fashioned dress,
And size, and claimed authority to excess.
In gift-offering processions, Number One
She must be, or taken back, undone,
Would be her charity. Of what use
Is such manner that is the caboose
Of Pride? Nor was spirituality
Sole aim of her pilgrimages abroad. Be
It said, they were also for the company
On pleasure trips. No devotee was she
In Jerusalem, in Roma, at any
Holy shrine abroad, or in her own country.
Very amused was I at her chit-chat
All the way to Georgia where this high-hat
And the other pilgrims left me to embark
On their long journey back to their bard.
Then lo! From the sky a shining star
Fell at my feet. This tale would be ajar,
Not come full circle, but for the entrance
Of the Parson I met: O Radiance
Of the Priesthood! His goodness, amen!
Esteemed, his faith in religion;

His unselfish dedication to work,
Untiring, wholly for his simple kirk.
His sweet songs do our hearts and Christus reach;
His love does Christian disunity breach.
He was, when we two met, so confident
Of a brand new friendship's establishment
That he said, indeed demanded outright
You must meet Virginia! Tell me what night.
Barely in the house where this came about,
Off came her shoes, which her dog trotted out
Just as the good Parson made his entrance
And was greeted in shoeless elegance.
As always is when two Irish get together,
They burst into song: lively, sad, and tender.
O sweet Georgia! O my friends and companions!
How lucky I am to have found *Jacob's Well*
In a strange land, and a Canterbury bell.

Celebrating
Dr. Virginia M. Meehan,
Chaucerian Scholar

DIVERGENT SISTERS

Destined from above
Was the love
That created us—
Children enabled,
By parents the same,
To partake
Of the same table.

A buzzing honeycomb
Was our home
With our mother
Providing the honey
—Not overly sweet,
Just sweet enough—
From nectar gathered
By our busy father.

They taught us—
Through their acts
Instead of words,
Which often tend
To bind the mind.

We were free!—
A stroke of genius!
For mystery
Left unspoken
Provoked in us
A soaring curiosity.

Later, we learned
To read the truth
In another's eyes,
And—sometimes—in books.
And so we grew, we two . . .

You looked like Father
And had our mother's ways;
I looked like Mother
And had our father's ways.

Were these the imprints
That made the difference?

You were ever gentle—
Soft like summer rain—
While I was oft—
Still am—a hurricane.

Yet constant remains
Our love for one another,
Consistent with the covenant—
Unspoken—with our mother.

Her honey, clinging to your feet,
Held you close to home. Nor,
When you married, did you roam,
But bought the house next door.

And soon it filled
With a handful of children—
Five in number—
Each gifted, each beautiful,
Fulfilling the dream
You dreamed with their father,
Sixty years ago.

Lo! The beauty of the tree
You planted with your husband . . .
It spreads its branches
Across the nation,
And yields its fruit—delicious!—
To the fourth generation.

To the Lord,
Who makes the tree
And builds the city,
You give all the glory
As you ought.

And it is He—
Our God—
Who marked us
Differently.

Each one of us, married—
Or single and living alone—
Carries His purpose for us
In a life uniquely our own.

He made you—
Loving another—
A mother of children . . .
He made me—
Living alone—
A creator of poems.

You, and your Love,
Provided the spendid newels—
Sturdy and strong—
To support the stair winding
Beyond the first-born star
To our Eternal Home . . .

While I—working alone—
Carpeted its steps
With my humble poems
To ease the feet
Of pilgrims daring
To climb those stairs
For a better view—
For the view at the top
So sublime!
Its beauty stops
The heart.

Of this, thank God,
I am a part.
Nor sterile,
Nor unfulfilled . . .

For my thoughts couple easily
With all who desire me;
With all, needing my balm,
Who find comfort in my arms.

In such affairs of mind
And heart, I do my part,
And lo!
The thrust of my thought
Generates new thoughts—diadems!
And the thrust of my jaw
Strengthens them.

I am not sterile—
I have children everywhere—
And royal!—upon this stair.

Yet . . .
All are figments
Of the imagination—
Torments!

For they are invisible,
While your children are visible.
You can touch them
And feel them.
You can put your arms around them.

How rich is your love!
And fertile
In your children
And in theirs.

While with greater insight,
I still write poems,
You stun our eyes
With the prize you've won!

For, even as we prepare
To sing our even-song,
You are adorned
With the most awesome
Gift of all . . .

For behold, today,
That winding staircase
Like the sun graced
In the Milky Way.

Behold! Behold!
How its newels
Sparkle like hosts
Of starry galaxies,
Their posts now embedded
With the family's
Most precious jewels.

For my sister
Elizabeth Magenheimer Bennison
and her husband
William Marcellus Bennison, Sr.,
on their 60th Wedding Anniversary
October 10, 1988

A FAIRY TALE

Once upon a time
Little Prince Martin, the seventh—
But the first Georgian-son
Of the King and Queen of Hearts

Journeyed with them
To the north country—
The land of his mother's birth—
To celebrate a family wedding.

And so it came to pass that Martin—
Hanging on the edge of a pew—
Never saw the radiant bride—
His mother's sister,
The Royal Princess Ann Marie—
But a flower girl caught his eye.

Confident in her three-year-old pride,
She marched self-consciously,
A little off center,
Strewing petals in the path of the bride.

The Georgian—himself full of charm—
Never saw so charming a sight;
Never saw a girl so pretty,
Never a girl with such pendulous hair!

With true southern grit,
He quickly claimed her at the reception
Where they danced every dance
Or walked around the hall
For all to see,
Their arms around each other.

Soon they were heard
To ask their grandfather
Couldn't they, too,
Get married that night?

Twice the little beauty—
A princess from Ohio
Called Gèneva—
Became capricious with her suitor,
Walking away,
Leaving him surprised
And speechless.

He threw his arms straight up,
Then down—
His face spoke volumes:
Women!

The second time she deserted him,
He moved to the table of the bride
And leaning his elbows on the edge,
Held his face in his hands—
A picture of utter dejection!

But quickly he was happy again.
When Gèneva coming beside him
Claimed a dance,
One would think
His heart had never been broken!

Later,
About to pose for a picture,
The prince took Gèneva's bouquet
From the nuptial table.

Then with all the courtliness
Of a Southern gentleman,
He presented it
To his little princess,
Telling her gently,
But quite firmly
As befits a man,

Here! Hold this!

They'd pose together—those two
Whose combined age was eight—
For the nearest thing
To a wedding portrait.

There had to be a climax
And it came late in the evening,
When Gèneva decided such devotion
Deserved her most generous guerdon.

Suddenly in the middle of a dance,
She threw her arms around him
And covered his face
With many and urgent kisses.

Abruptly Martin freed himself,
Turned his back on the lady
And, shaking his head in disbelief,
Walked away.

As he passed near my table,
I heard him say
I can't stand it!
It's too much for me!
I just can't stand it!

* * * * *

Almost ten years have taken flight
Since that magical night.
The prince is fifteen—
Blue-eyed and blond—
And stands six foot one.

No girl as yet
Has captured his heart.
His first love is the trumpet;
His second is his spinet.

And on the threshold of womanhood
Stands Gèneva of the long, long
Golden tresses.
Blue blue are her eyes,
Sparked by her innate intelligence.
And her beauteous face is animated
By her natural curiosity
About all things above, below,
In and on the waters and the earth.

Now, at thirteen,
The whirr of propellers
Attracts her. This summer,
Flying through the air,
She will leave all future suitors grounded
Until—like Rapunzel—she lets down
Her glorious, pendulous hair.

For my grandniece and my grandnephew
Gèneva Barbara Conaway-Bennison
and Martin Steven Couch;
and for my niece
Ann Marie Bennison Pavona,
the bride who furnished
the setting for this tale

A FOUR-MONTHS-OLD FETUS CARRIED ACROSS CAMPUS IN A PLASTIC BAG

Who is this poet who lies here
Petrified, denied even the first clear
Note of its song?

Who, the scientist whose shrivelled
Hands can now cure no ill
Nor ever swirl a test tube?

Who, the plasterer, the painter,
The plumber—aye! the peacemaker
Needed to order our chaos?

Who is it who floats
Face down, an inverted footnote
At the bottom of a page?

His ears, his eyes,
His mouth, like butterflies,
Already adhere

To his head, his face fashioned
Like none other and once impassioned
Just for being.

There! See his arms, his legs, his hands
        delicate as rainbows:
His feet, his fingers, and O! his toes
Near ready to go to market.

Only growth was needed to grace,
To shape out his structure already in place;
To finely tune his nerves.

With him was a galaxy of gifts wrapped
        in plastic
And packaged by a string so drastic,
Unknown—utterly unknown—

Will be his love, his laughter, his soul—
All stilled forever in alcohol . . .
All *lifeless* in a plastic bag.

A GOLDEN GIFT
To a Single Mother-to-be

O Star-crossed Woman!
Not once, but twice
You have hidden
Your tears.
Not once, but twice
Your heart has been broken.
Yet, as in the first while,
You smile that glorious smile!

Who can guess, then, the halves
Of a heart turned granite;
Or feel on its frozen walls—
As on memorials of war—
The carved glyptographs
Of your unframed pain.

Who can know how *cold*
You were in August, or September,
That caused your tender flower
To bend—to unfold—

Before that hot, humid wind:
The sirocco *(rien de beau!)*
That picked up moisture

As from the southeast
It did blow
Across your lonely sea
Into Italy.

Who could judge your need to know
If ever again you could feel that warmth—
O Heaven Incognito!—
That, through a merciful God,
Followed Adam and Eve
Out of Eden, to be
Divine benevolence to our exile;
A remembrance of Paradise.

God Himself felt an abandoned man;
Alone, as you have been alone,
Since that malignant night
Deprived you of your bridal rites, and bed,
When you and your true love were to wed.

Enough of sorrow! said the Lord, then
Let a wild seed drift in that wind
To carry a precious gift—
His gift to you—
Of flesh and blood: *your* flesh and bone
To be your Love, your very own,
Nor ever again will you be alone!

Special is this child who, even now,
Finds welcome shelter in your inn,
Close to a heart that now obtains
More joy than ever it could contain.

Golden is this child with eyes,
Sapphirine perhaps, wherein—it is hoped—
Will be found that mischievous imp
That so intrigued a poet, many years ago,
(Were you only two?)
In your blue and crystal eyes.

JOSEPH EDWARD CARLSON

From God you are come, little one,
The guardian of your parents' love,
Now fabulously enriched since you left
Your home with God

To share with your mother and father
Your ten little toes and fingers—
So perfect!—to be smothered
All over with kisses that linger,

Like ghosts of sweet love, in the air.
Anxiously, they await your smile—
Your first! At *them!* What can compare
With this enchantment, this lack of guile?

Warmly your parents and your grandparents
Welcome you, dear Joseph, to your home
On earth, for it is apparent
That you've come forth from a honeycomb.

Now, in God's family you take your place,
Armed with His love and shield divine;
For today He fills you with His grace
And marks you with the Christian sign.

For Joseph Edward's Baptism
January 3, 1982

HEAT WAVE IN GEORGIA

Seared on the memory
Of Georgians forever
Are these fiercely hot days,

When Apollo,
Sending a plague into their camp,
Sets fire to their tents
And blackens their fields;
Withers their crops
And burns their beasts.

Who would believe this
Of so flawless a youth?
Apollo must be *stoned*,
It's said;
And further said,
Since all men are confident
Of his protection,
How could this paragon
Of manliness
Turn into such a
Raging pyromaniac?

Who would believe it?

Hasn't he come
From a wise and glorious home?
Is he not revered?
Apollo Belvedere!

Nowhere is there relief
From his punishment—
So severe now,
Georgia groans
Into the breathless air.
And cries of mourning rise
For those who find sudden death
In his eyes.

Too long now
Georgians have been stunned
By the terrible barrage
Of his arrows.
They cry,
Is there no one on Olympus
Who will put him
Behind a cloud for a while
And bring him to his senses?

O *God*, pray the swooning Georgians,
Thou Who dost reign
Over the sun and the moon,
Come to our aid!

Do Thou put Apollo
Behind a cloud; and send us,
Please send us
Some rain.

THE GENERATOR

Sprung as I was from a
Limited soil, I swayed
On shallow roots: a sapling—
Until a passerby,
Aware of a tree's
Unique vocation, poured
Her blood into my starved soil
And stirred
My first leaf to life.

For that rare,
most powerful teacher:
the one who inspires.

GRAINNE
AN IRISH WOLFHOUND

Grainne could not remember
Nor know, by name, September or December.
But in a monologue, peculiar to a dog,
She lay claim (with Irish impulsion
And a special sound for little ones)
To boys and men: and to children—spellbound
At the sight, all-hail!
Of a wagging tail.

Flagstaff and flag combined
Waved greetings—undefined, instinctive—
From a heart inarticulate,
Indiscriminate, being captive
Of outstretched hands
And her master's gentle commands.

Had he taught her to be aware
Of the posture of prayer? . . .

For death found her
Today
Kneeling beside his bed:
Her hind legs bent, and on its spread
Lay her head . . .

Her heart fixt, and confident
At leaving her pups
To the love she knew . . .

And knows now, again,
In her new master, Francis. The Assisian.

For the children of
Our Lady of Perpetual Help Parish
Carrollton, Georgia,

and Grainne's seven beautiful pups.

KINSHIP

Look! *Look* at trees!
Observe in their leaves
The beginning of life
And its end.

After slumber,
In spring and summer
Colored green like youth—
Uniform.

Who then foresees
In young men or trees—
Both whose bent depends on
Storms and sun—

The rhapsody
Of autumn's glory
Celebrating in red
Brown and gold

The poetry
Of life's liturgy
Before the white, deep sleep
Of winter?

So too all men
In the season when—
With tired sap dropping
In their limbs—

Like trees, become
A delirium
Of color—their walk, talk,
Their faces

Fired anew—
And in hue
Endlessly divergent—
Distinctive—

Ere nature
Returns men to dust
And conformity like
Winter's trees.

MOON-WALKER
and Her Mother

A rune you were—a sweet mystery—
Until your mother saw
The moon rising in your eyes . . .
A riddle unguessed
Until—brushing your hair—
She discovered moondust in the air.

O Heaven-sent child—
Whose phosphorescent smile
Tugs at her heart
Like the moon pulling tides—

No less overcome is she
To see that frown
Tweaking your brow . . .
The lights idling
In your big brown eyes
Like the moon twiddling its thumbs
Behind the back of a passing cloud.

So clued, it must be true
Before you stepped on earth,
You first stepped on the moon!

There, no meadow-pink grew,
No bobolink sang . . .
And oh, little astronaut,
How unfeeling—cold!—
How mirthless was its goddess
Who kept her bow-string taut,
Her arrows twanging
Against the man or god
Who'd even think of love.

Then indeed, Diana's missiles
Sped after you, dear Jessica,
When—seeking love—
You fled to earth . . .

There, no riches
Awaited your daring birth—
No golden chariot, sweet nymph,
Nor stags with antlers of gold.

Yet—from God Himself—
You found the greatest treasure:
Love unmeasured
In your mother's boundless heart.

And now—so soon?—
A toddler you've become . . .
Wildly frolicking with another
And quite overcoming your mother.

Yet nothing gives her
A pleasure more exquisite
Than watching how you walk
From room to room—around—

Not really walking
But—your legs like pogo sticks—
Springing up and down . . .
As if you were still walking
On the moon.

For my great-grandniece
Jessica Lynn Germinario Brady
18 months old.

THE MAYPOLE

Let us celebrate life,
Whose days—
While always the same
To the old—
Are ever green
To the young . . .

Who, day after day,
Dance around its pole
Like the Queen of the May,
Whose steps—

Although repetitious
In their circling
And going nowhere,
'Round and 'round—

Yet entrance us
With, not the best,
But ah, the sweetest
Of remembrance.

*MY ANGEL SHALL GO BEFORE YOU**

The winter fields were sleeping, dreaming spring,
While stars were sleepwalking, wide-eyed, behind
The clouds that cluttered up the bed of night
In rumpled rolls, a puckered blanket spread
Across the sky from which the lights had fled.

The road became a narrow hall sans walls;
The only flashlight: the headlights that pierced
And searched the darkness like a burglar's torch
As nimble-footed rubber thieves advanced
And cased the miles along the scary road.

This was the last of Christmas holidays:
We'd played the palm-dotted, sun-spangled state
And window-shopped along Miami's streets.
We'd laughed with dolphins, frowned on sharks
        and teased,
From trees, macaws who winked or swooped
        at us.

The hours we'd driven home were mingled
        laughs
With honeycombed talk of leagued kin
        and friends.
Now thirty minutes more or less from home,
We knew the welcome waiting: warm, complete.
No place like home, we sang; and sang again.

Suddenly!
Without warning lights,
Our eyes picked up
A loaded truck,
Swarming with logs,
Stuck, *stopped dead ahead,*
Blocking the narrow road.

Instantly!
The tune died in our throats.
Horrified, my friend cried,
"My God!
We're going to hit!"
No sooner said, when

CRASH!

CRACK!!

CRUNCH!!!

* * * * *

The fouled street quivered at once
With ashen spooks
Curious about the ruinous truck.
Each one
Looked at the wreck;
Each one
Shivered weirdly
At a dark and veering cloud
Flecked with blood.

I did not think of Him then
Just stared
At the spider's web
Cracking the windshield;
And followed
Each crooked crack
As it spread
Across the field of glass.

And stared
Through it
At lethal logs
Just inches in default of my head
When—Oh God! What luck!—
The car screeched
To a jarred halt
Underneath the truck.

Stared
In total disbelief:

Why aren't we dead?

I did not think of Him
Until they'd drawn up my legs.
Then I thought

". . . they have numbered all my bones."**

And Christ's pain pelted the plains,
Harshly,
Like sharpened shards of icy sleet.

Remembering
December 29, 1978,
at Newnan, Georgia

*Ex 23,23.
**Ps 21,18.

NIGHT INTRUDERS

The sun not yet breaks
The winter sky
When, suddenly, I lie
Wide awake.

Eye-balled to darkness.

Listen! Triple sighs,
Insidious in the same key,
Breathe outside my bedroom door . . .
My heart petrifies.

Who's that?!!

How know,
Just from sleep,
The furnace rondo
Disposed by zero cold?

As if this were not enough,

These adolescent walls
Are frightened thieves
Cracking their knuckles
Along the frozen eaves.

Benighted once again,
My heaped up dreams are mobbed . . .
My sleep, unbuckled,
Robbed.

OBSERVING SAMUEL BECKETT OBSERVE AN OLD COUPLE

O snide Sam Beckett! How you do deride
The aging wife with that silly hat you
Mis-ally with her furrowed face while the weight
Of her years, grasping her waist, holds her fast.

You ridicule her taste, dressing her
In the relic of her last dance: a gown
Now exposing shriveled arms and chicken-neck,
And clowning, abandoned, unpointed breasts.

To remind her that she is at ebb-tide,
You give her a molecule of toothpaste
To brush her teeth. Cruel man! This and lipstick
Are the life-lines that hold her to the shore.

But to her purblind husband you are kinder,
Mister Beckett: You keep him out of sight
Except for the back of his head, on which
He angles his hat with a defiant pat.

In contrast to her tools of vanity,
You give him a newspaper whose rustling
Indicates his mind is alert, albeit
Solely to sports and wars and politics.

She is a chatter-box at whom he grumbles
Brusquely, more often absent-mindedly.
When irked by the sound of her voice,
        the old man
Crawls into a hole and, eloquently silent,

Refuses her the comfort of his grunts
On which she relies, at the least, for company.
And—perhaps because she never sees him—
She begs to know that he is near, alive!

Yet she savors each day
Made happy—for want of better things—
By little things. For these,
And for the day itself,

She fervently thanks God—
Indeed! Just for a new day—
And glorifies Him
World without end.

And she prays her ever wistful hope
That the man will climb
Around their separation
And just once more—*just once more!*—

Come within her sight so that she may see him
As once she had when their love was young
And had no need for words.
Oh! *That* would be a happy day!

Feverishly, she paints her lips and files her nails,
Then plays a little music box:
There is something she remembers,
        and she smiles:
Phlox and petunia border this day!

But oh! How many times past had she
        been tempted
To kill that man! And yet, this perfumed day
Pre-empts the reason why she kept the gun,
Cast from her now; cast far away.

Then the years, mounting higher and higher,
Clutch her throat. She cannot speak.
        Her life-lines
Float out to sea. And yet, she prays
        for the sight,
Just one more time, of that arbitrary man.

Too late, and yet in time
Before she is swept into the Eternal Sea,
The old man—responding to some mysterious
Prod (her prayers?)—

Crawls out of his hole
And, striving mightily, noisily hauls himself
On hand and knee over the mountain
Of his self-entrenched acerbity.

At last, he lies before her, exhausted
But out of reach, alas! Wide-eyed, he stares

In disbelief. Rejoice, O Happy Day!
He is there, once more, within her sight.

She sees his apprehension, his stricken look.
And notes his slow, shocked comprehension
That no longer will he hear her voice;
That she is finally leaving him. She beams:

This *is* a happy day!

Upon watching, on PBS,
Samuel Beckett's "Happy Days"

ON READING CERTAIN—
NOT *ALL*, THANK GOD!—
LOVE POEMS OF ROD MCKUEN

Deep in our heads
Burns the phallus
Become Rome.
Burns bright
A room
Become Colosseum.

We are
Deceived,
Taken in
By your bold
Imagines.

Now, one remembers
The decadent City
Obsessed too with thighs and breasts.
Its own foreskin.
Its lump,
At last, its cancer.

And that colossal
Antiquity:
Noxious circle compressed
With bad sweat

Exuding from armpit, sperm,
Stale blood, insanity.

Except, perhaps,
Your loves—One? Two?
All?—
Who turned
Away.

THE DRUG ADDICT AND HIS MOTHER

She remembers a child's caprice;
His smile, a passport
To the land of Greece
Or was it . . . King Arthur's Court?

His shy returns. Surprise
Of wild flowers
And four-year-old eyes
Easily absolved for anxious hours.

Aye! Golden in time and synthesis,
The years since he was born . . .
Without warning then, their nemesis
Of silence filled with sudden scorn.

Now, his face turns
From his own here on earth.
At "love" fests, he publicly spurns
The Love that gave him birth.

She stares incredibly into the looking-glass.
My son! My son! Wherefore this betrayal?
A mother's cry splintering heaven. Alas!
There is no answer . . . no return from Baal.

LAMENT

Cry! Cry, my soul,
For that pulverized rock,
Once a mountain's lofty peak.
Quartz. Crystal!
Struck broadside
By the sun's rising sword.
O *Iridescent Light:*
Whereto your beauty!

P'AN-KU, CONFUCIUS, AND THE MODERN WORLD

(Impressions from a study of Asian Civilization)

From the roofless sky
By night and by day,
P'an-ku's soft moon-eye
And his great, burning sun-eye—
Shocked at what they behold
On the blue planet—
Turn and shiver
In their sockets.

Tears then, too heavy to hold back,
Give way,
As they did so long ago,
And flood anew
The Yangtze River
And churn the mud
In the Yellow.

China is old—
Very, very old—
But to this day,
This tale is told:

Just as his eyes
Upon his death
Became the sun and the moon,
So too,
P'an'ku's breath
Became the freezing wind
Blown from the North.
And in the South,
The plants came forth
From his greening hair.

And Five Sacred Mountains
Stretched from his whitened bones
And enthroned themselves
At the icy foot of heaven.

His words,
The legend goes,
Cracked like thunder
From their rugged walls
And rumbled through
That most awesome world
Where all things—
As if a ghost had spoken—
Succumbed to that eerie,
Unending sound.

And when this fear
Redounded upon P'an'ku,
His racked flesh—
Become now the water
In all the ponds and streams—
Crawled to the coast
To fill the seas.

From out of this myth,
China's proud civilization arose
Under the divine impetus
Of her own yellow Emperor,
Who—with the aid of his sovereign Lady—
Rolled back the unpolished stone.

And the shroud,
Left behind in the ancient tomb,
Survives to this day
With the imprints of China's genius,
In all but the law,
Miraculously intact.

But there are those
Who would hold society hostage:
Graceless, uncouth men—
The terrorists of their day—
Bent on the destruction
Of every good in their heritage.
And China was no exception.

Happily, China never lost her soul,
For she held most holy
The Sacrament of Education
First celebrated, ritually,
By Confucius,
Who believed that
Under the consecrated elements
Of China's past wisdom,
Peace was truly present.

Well may P'an'ku deplore
Modern Man's strange confusion:
At odds with himself,
He is estranged
From the wisdom
Of his past.

Ignored was
The tortoise shell
That had washed up
On his shore.

On it, he might have found inscribed
This Confucian oracle:

Learning without thought
Is labour lost.

For Professor Floyd E. Hoskins
on his retirement, 1978,
from West Georgia College.

LAUREN

At last—O Miracle of Birth!—
A baby thrusts its fern-covered head
And long, fragile stem
Through that warm red earth;
And now lies, like a flower,
In the bed of her mother's arms.

O little girl, you are
Already endowed with power
To conquer hearts and, with the
Essence of God's own breath,
To sweeten the world
With His presence.

Charmed at the sight of her,
Two married lovers,
All eyes and hushed beyond words,
Marvel
At their Word made flesh.

For Lauren Theresa Germinario

A POET MAKES A POEM

Open-air trolleys
Are my thoughts,
Turning round and round
On the turntable
Of my mind,
Being readied to fulfill
Their destiny atop
Inspiration Hill.

For now, yet steadied as it goes,
There is the sound
Of a dull bell found
In the opening line.

But soon the bell will peal
With its wondrous appeal
As it reveals its aspiration
For the star
But dimly sighted at the start.

For this while
And for a while,
My thoughts erupt
In fits and starts.
The wheels squeak
And the bell clangs—
Bangs and clangs—

As I grope my way up
That green and purple slope.

Nor do I, nor will I, stop
Until I reach the very top.

There the view
Strikes the eye
Suddenly, like sunlight
When fog lifts,
When rain stops.

Full of glorious glory
And with its beauty fixed,
Is this moment
When the poem
Completes.

Fully born,
It then becomes
The golden gate
Connecting hearts
And them to me,
Who would envision
For the inarticulate,
For those who cannot express
And hardly address
The longings, so mysterious,
Deep within the heart.

Somehow, someway,
A poem is a highway
To the region of the gods.
It connects us on earth,
And Earth to Heaven,
Like the bridge, all golden,
Connects to San Francisco.

Indeed, this I know,
And intimately so—

I myself
Am San Francisco.

GENIE AND ST. SIMONS ISLAND

At the edge of the humid isle
Now claimed as your own,
The refreshing, tumescent sea
Alleged its right to your heart.
Alleluia! you cried, *I'm home!*

You explored the moss
Embossing oaks,
Touched the mold on ancient tombs,
Then cuffed your breath!
Here was death with its ghosts
Cloaked in mystery and plumed!

What a find for a writer: Sea!
Sand! And ghosts!
Engrailing that Golden Isle,
You fleshed the bones of the dead,
Freed their speech and loosened their looks,
And made books
Of their history's untold tales.

For my friend,
Eugenia Price

WITHOUT TEARS

This is grief: the heart shuttered for voices
Struck dumb. O Zachariac unbelief!
Oh, the vacuum left now that the Reaper
Has harvested grasses that greened and ripened
By your side and sweetened the air, the field
you shared.

This is grief: the memory of fragrance
No longer to be inhaled in great gulps,
Filling up the nose and lungs to satisfy
The heart's vague longing for those familiar
scents—
Aromatic then, and now so pleasing to God.

That Heaven is enhanced by their essence
Is God's consolation to those bereaved,
Whose tenacious faith instructs their splintered
hearts;
But none to those buffeted by the wild winds
That assailed Millay, who cried *I am not resigned.*

O attestor of God's steadfast love
And comforter of the afflicted,
Your own tears must go unshed

To keep unscathed your gift
To water arid hearts;
To slake the thirst
For our beloved dead.

He helped others, they said
At the foot of the Cross,
Himself He cannot save.

We pray for you,
Dear twice-struck friend,
Who, craving the sweet
Smell of those grasses,
Must hang there now . . .
Without tears.

Remembering the strength of Eugenia Price in her successive bereavements shortly after the appearance of her 1982 book *Getting Through the Night*— her gift to those who mourn.

REMARKS ON FRIENDSHIPS AND ON OURS

The lips are the wombs—
Or tombs—of friendships—

For it is talk
That brings them to birth
And ever, thereafter,
Nourishes them—
And tops its feasts
With delicious laughter.

Ah, talk!—
How dependent on its worth
Is friendship's enrichment . . .
How detrimental is its dearth.

And now—
Having made these observations—
This poet would celebrate
Those whose spirit—
Like ours—
Is animated by good conversations.

Stimulating—
Like the caress
Of a lover—
Is the unending talk
Between such friends.

No less, then,
Than love's expectation
Is their anticipation
Of delightful discoveries
As they walk
Toward the light
In one another.

Yet, out of mutual respect
(And better than lovers do),
They safeguard the space
Sacred to the other—
Which yields
An unexpected dividend . . .

For the friendship
Most securely bound
Is found to be
Most truly free.

Comfortable, then—
And joyful!—
Are their togethers
When they pull and shred
And twist anew
Threads of knowledge
From the other's spool
To wind upon their spindles . . .

A little cottage industry
Showing a profit—a mystery!—
For no one comes
Through their door
To buy or sell
What cannot be bought
Or sold—
The ribbons of wisdom
Lying on the floor.

Nor can boredom enter
This kingdom
(Indeed! It is banished!),
Where the mind is mined
In search for treasure.
And *this*
Is pleasure!

As priceless as the art
In the Vatican gallery
(And dearer to them by far)
Is the uppermost part
Of their castle, which—
Structured by design
For its finest view—
They call their *belvedere.*

How clear, from there,
Is their view
Of each other's opinion
Unobstructed
By imperiousness.

For here,
In all seriousness,
They can discuss—or argue,
If they must—totally free
To agree or disagree . . .

A tribute—supreme!—
To their courtesy
That—unpinioned—
Springs naturally
And radiantly
From a dignity
Innate and serene.

Only on these wings
Can a thought fly with ease—
Unhooded—
Like the sharp-eyed hawk
Upon release
From its falconer's wrist.

The gods do smile on them
For this. And for this—

For while their thinking
Bears no tinkering,
They are the kind of folk
Who harbor in their hearts
Those mischievous imps
Forever concocting a joke
To play on one another . . .

A gift beyond compare—
For laughter brings relief
Like the relief of prayer.

So does friendship grow
Between spirits kindred
Such as they—
Who know that Time himself
Makes their cloak.

And oh, they know
Its unique beauty
Depends upon the cloth
He weaves
From yarns that only they
Can spin for him.

Ah, how comfortable
Is the cloak we wear! . . .
How smooth the cloth—
And rare.

You notice? You are aware
That I did not mention
That thread—divine—
That gives our cloak
Its golden shine? . . .

The unselfish dimension
Of our friendship's
Noble, restful love?

It is, my Friend,
Beyond my pen.

But look!
You will find it
Everywhere
Between these lines.

It is there . . .
It is simply there.

For Mary Anne Goreau de Villier

A VALENTINE FOR CARROLLTON

From Boston town to Athens' Parthenon,
Flesh and blood—family, friends, oh! dear lovers!—
Were my only loves. Thought I another
Never was, until I came to Carrollton.

Such pity had I for Horace, who thought
At fifty years he was too old for love.
Not I! Once gone, quickly I was caught
By Cupid's arrows with another love,

Never guessing that impish god held
The very best 'til last. O blithe, dear Shade
Of Horace! Dost know I—unparalleled
Save for thine—do have a Sabine farm? Eh?

Where I contemplate woodland and vines;
Eat cheese, young onions, olives—anything
That found its origin in Rome. And wine!
Not from bowls Falernian, yet for kings.

In my garden there is mint, and a tired,
Fallen tree. There grows ivy for my hair,
For 'tis there the muse does string my lyre.
What more, I ask, can my beating heart bear:

The weeping cherry tree that every spring
Traces my eyes with its delicate grace?
The lemon-scented tree astonishing
Me with each magnolia's lovely face?

Atlanta, Horace, is my Rome: I yield
To forays there, and even farther roam,
Knowing that here awaits my driving-wheel:
The quiet solitude of my home.

Here I find contentment. Nor am disinclined
To share with friends a rousing party
In homes more simple or more rich than mine—
Shining! Lighted bright by love's Astarte.

Dear Roman, I agree: The last is best!
Sabine was yours; mine, Georgia's rolling hills.
Though pate with silver, I am golden-tressed!
Horace, sprung, before spring, are daffodils!

SNOW DRIFTING

Nor rhyme nor reason
Explains this drifting snow.
The flaming season
Is but just now upon us.

O! Indian givers are the hours! For her,
The harsh end of the year is here.
Her body already shivers
From winter's freezing showers.

Her breath defaults to the north wind.
Ice snaps apart
Under the halting
Steps of her heart

Even as

God skips joyously over flagons of wine,
Abetting pleasure-trips across vespertine skies;
Dripping cognac and yellow champagne,
        and ohhh!
Clarets and apricot brandy on trees below . . .

Intoxicating, exhausting autumn-beauty—
Intimation of her apocalypse
When, at last, He wipes away the frost
From her lips.

For my beloved aunt, Elizabeth Klein,
During crisis, October 5, 1976

THE WIDOWED MOTHER AND THE VIRGIN

Side by side, blushing
On the gleaming altar cloth,
Lie two red roses

While the bride and groom,
Before God and man, recite
Their nuptial vows.

Beside the father,
Who gives his daughter away,
Sways her proud mother;

While across the aisle,
The bridegroom's widowed mother
Sits alone, and smiles . . .

Nor can anyone guess
How her heart, twice deprived,
Fears her empty nest.

Like a bird at her ear,
She hears—and would stop!—
The Holy Lesson's word:

Wherefore a man
Shall leave father and mother
And shall cleave to his wife.

Yes! Raising a son
For another family
Is every parent's

Destiny. Christmas
Will never be the same, nor
Any holiday.

'Tis then the Virgin
Comes to chide, comfort
The pale-eyed woman:

I was a widow
When my Son left me doubly
Bereft. I saw Him go

And knew not where
Until I beheld Him there—
Dead upon a cross.

So why do you pine?
Your sorrow is not like mine.
Your son goes forth to life!

And as our Lady
Leaves, oh so sweet a fragrance
Fills the holy room.

And such is the transport
Of the widow's heart, so numb
Before, she kisses

Her thumb to God's Mother:
Gracias, she murmurs,
Gracias! Madre de Dios!

And closes her eyes
To pray: For today her son
Goes forth to life

To glorify his father's name.

For my Peruvian-American friend
Isabel Rios Hubbell

MARY PAYNE WILLIAMS

At Eighty Years

Ha! She could hardly walk
And rarely did she talk
Save with her smile while
The men—both young and old—
Lined up for their golden chance
To dance with her.

TO EACH HIS OWN

She is skinny, graceless:
This pale creature
With no breasts

And no charm,
Not even in her eyes
Kept shuttered against the world.

Her voice-box
Ejects splinters
Like sticks scratched together

But never long enough
To flame
And give warmth.

Or so her neighbors thought
Until a black man moved in
And became her lover.

Fie! Fie! they cry,
Denying
Her hunger.

Instead, they wonder
If she had been ignored
As a child

And broke other children's toys
To attract
Attention?

THE WATERING-HOLE

Softly
The sound of the piano
Stole through the forest
Of tastes and satisfied adult
Animals of every stripe
Who stood, knee-deep,
In the watering-hole
Grunting to each other
Between long, bracing drinks.

It was then that those
Feeling winter in their bones
Requested the *September Song*
But that proved too sobering
And quickly groaned
To its eternal rest.

The sentimental Irish
Seized the moment of demise
And sang *Danny Boy*
Through grieving pipes
Clogged with tears.
Then, fortified once more
With the solace of their peculiar wakes,
They flogged the air
With their *Wild Irish Rose.*

And all the animals
Felt better; even I,
The only puppy there,
Who barked like a prairie dog.

The great, brooding cat,
Pawing at the keyboard,
Caught the mood
And shook his mane:
At last, at that,
The chase was on!

He was, far and away,
The lion of the party,
Leaping and crashing
Down on the piano;
Sure-footed on every note—
Calculated to flush out
His prey: the libido
Hidden away
In these proud, secret animals.

Dum, da da, da, da da.
Dum, da da, da, da da.
Dum, dum, dum, dum.
Dum, dum, dum, dum.
DUM . . . DUM . . .
DUM . . . DUM . . .
DUM!!!

The lion roared as he
Scented primeval passions
Cached against the need
Of academe;
Beneath the false face of the politic
The typed face of the entrepreneur.

For there were there
Animals of every stripe:

The bulls and bears
With their blood
Pressured by the stock market.
Sheep guarded by their watch-dogs,
The dumb ox, a dodo or two—
The meat of sharper animals—
And calfless cows.
And bull-less cows.
And bitches, with or without the less
Exciting hounds.
And—bow us down!—the Lord-mayor fox.

Also, accompanied by their does,
The self-wise and otherwise Ph.D.-stags,
Whose heads came up suddenly
At the slightest sortie
Into their territory.

And there were gentle ewes,
Fresh from their mangers,
Who looked on calmly
Sensing no danger.

And the dissolute boars,
Notorious for their insatiable thirst,
Constantly sniffing and rooting out
With their telling snouts
The fifth and more of gin.

Towering over all was
The long-necked giraffe
(And his long-necked better-half),
Who wanted so much to unbend.
Alas! His head had been in the trees too long.

The tagging puppy
Ensnared him with a wagging tale;
And forthwith it was seen
That his stiff neck bent slightly,
That his ears twitched.
More! It was allowed by all
That a giraffe could laugh out loud.

Dum, dum, dum, dum.
Dum, dum, dum, dum:

Just enough to start hands drumming—
Feet inclining too—
Just enough for behinds to start swaying,
Wiggling—even those, some would say,
Undesigned for wiggling.

DUM . . . DUM . . .
Dum, da da, da . . . da da.
Dum, da da, da . . . da da.

The animals were shaking their tails.

DUM . . . DUM . . .
DUM . . . DUM . . .

And now more emphatically.

The final, irresistible DUM!!!
Brought them to their feet
And they danced around and bumped around
On their hind legs—an amazing feat!

The giraffes should have stayed for the fun,
For all at once
The animals—one and all—
Fell down, laughing,
Into a heated heap.

The puppy let out a yelp
As she curled herself up in a corner
And dreamed of her prowling ancestors
In those far-off whore-house days
That added the "Wild" to the West.

She stood and shook herself alert
Just as the exhausted hostess—the greyhound
Who'd been racing spinach balls and appetites—
Bounded into the jungle

Twirling her telltale belt
(Bea Lillie twirling her rope of pearls)
And gave at the end of her runway
The grandest delaying bump of all.

No stripper ever eased a bump with more finesse.
Here was, indeed, a work of art
Whose liveliness outstripped her paintings
Frozen—for just that moment—to the
overarching trees.

By the way, the eminent giraffes
Should have stayed at the watering-hole.
Oh! How fey they'd have been
(Third definition or even the first)
When the saints came marching in.

For my friends
Martha and Henry Setter

WIND SONG

Wind Song: the sight of trees.
The smell of sassafras.
Firey sunsets. Rain-soaked clouds.
White wisps of dried out clouds—
Crisp lace curtains on
The window of the sky.

Wind Song:
A flageolet whose flutelike
Music
Mutes a soul's loud cry.

A TOAST TO A BRIDE-TO-BE

Probably we misjudged—
It was so many years ago—
But wasn't that you we saw
Stealing from your mother's kitchen
With a handful of goodies
She intended for us?

No excuse had I—it was bridge night—
For trumping my partner's ace,
Except, out of the corner of my eye,
I saw your lovely face
And thought that even as a child
You must be driving little boys wild!

However the others survived,
There was one boy so smitten
His love for you was crystalized
The moment you set your eyes on him.

The boy's name was *Kevin.*
And—happy for this day—
He struck a spark within your heart;
You fell in love with him.

Let us celebrate Love—
Your love—for Love
Is birthed in Heaven
To be consummated on earth.

And so, before we dine,
We lift to you—
And to Kevin, here in spirit—
A glass of wine.

May your love grow
Like the tendrils of April
May all your troubles fade away
Like snow in the month of May!

For Anne Marie Sanders,
Bride-elect of J. Kevin Worley

MY GUARDIAN ANGEL

Her spirit rises in beauty
Like the violet *Africana*
Sitting on its lover's windowsill
Content with the sunlight

Filtering through the bays
Like candlelight reflecting
From the February throats
Dependent on St. Blase.

Her skin—caramelized
As if by burnt sugar—
Is a smooth and satiny surprise.
And her merry dark eyes
Dance and flicker
Like the night skies
Over Africa.

Her name is Lunell,
Meaning love.

She is an astral lamp,
So designed and self-designed
That her light casts no shadow
On her table . . .

Nor do those of her children—
All beautiful and capable,
All stamped with the monogram
Of her love.

This was the gift given her
By the wee little Lamb when—
But five days out of the womb—
She was left a motherless child

As her birth mother,
Leaving the earth,
Went out
With the morning tide.

She is the keeper of my home,
Humming as she works,
Unfurling flags of laughter
As—armed with dusters and her mops—
She marches through the house.

She is my friend in need,
And wise. She is God-sent,
Tending me when I'm well
And when I'm sick.

She is my eyes, my walking stick . . .
My guardian angel
Loving me,
            Guiding me,
                        Watching over me.

For Lunell Addison,
My friend whom I love.

Photo by Bachrach

KM in Greenwich Village

1935

at 27

Part II

CLOUD OF THE UNKNOWN

(Legacy of Sappho)

for B. T.

LEGACY OF SAPPHO

The world laughs at this love.
Why not laugh
At a baby's helpless cries;
Or the pain in some mother's eyes?

The world mocks this love
With a stinging word.
Would it mock
The cry of a wingless bird?

HOW IT STARTED

A sweet madness,
Extruding thin white threads of pain,
Filled all the room last night—
A spider spinning a web
To ensnare us.

THE RETURN GIFT

The sea, the sky, the stars excited us.
We laughed at Larinae-sentries half asleep
on mildewed pilings.
Salt-air exhilarated us—as did music, and
dancing, and quarreling.

Love would have given a quiet joy

When I brushed by you, a light flamed in your
eyes.
When I sat reading, you crossed the room
And straddled my heart with your loneliness.

Love would have held out its arms

Your pain found a refuge in my own;
And day after day and night after night
You stole my strength and time.

Love would have given them willingly

I was troubled by the wild, hot aimlessness
of you
Bearing down on my mind and spirit
With its dissipation.

Love would have been your hand in mine

I did not ask for you; nor you for me.
I was a prop to strengthen your spirit;
        and props are not forever.
Your own heart and I warned you of this.

Love knows no warnings

Days of more than a year passed, the nights too.
Constant trespass gives possession: I had to give
        you back your loneliness.
Now, I see two holes where your eyes used to be.

Love's eyes shine like water in the sun

I had wrapped a gift for you: You can stand alone
        now, resolute as I knew you would.
What I did not expect was a gift from you
        in return: the two holes in your face—
So that I cannot remember now what first dried
        your tears, nor the flight of a seagull
        through your eyes.

Only Love remembers such things.

PSYCHE UNCERTAIN

Begging for love,
I give to you
Thoughts swift as a swallow;
Grey, wise as a dove.

Often plain as a sparrow,
Colorless;
Sometimes having the grace
Of a swan on water.

These things I give to you,
I know:

Rose-sheened
Myrtle
With fragrant flowers—
Leaves evergreened.

Silence
In the heart
Of a
Rose.

Sweet, juicy
Pomewater
Like the one
That tempted Eve.

With showy,
Scarlett
Poppy dreams,
I often make you drowsy.

But do not touch
The pine knots at
The end of my torch
With impunity. Such

Is my pole—
And you have endured enough.
Sheathe
Your soul,

Or you may yet moil
A hideous monster
Whose shoulder quivered
With your sweet, hot oil.

But if you do not gird
A creature with golden wings,
What will become of you—
Fluttering like a bird?

AH! BE STILL A MOMENT

I cupped my hands
To drink at your spring,
But your waters escaped
Through my fingers,

Leaving me
Disquieted;
Unquenched;
Disparate.

PRESCIENCE

We were sitting at the kitchen table
Marveling at the forsythia spilling
Its golden fountains over the yard,
Saying that the lilac bush there at the open
        window
Would soon send its purple fragrance
        through the house.

We were at home with the silver-toned words
That passed between us like an outstretched hand.
Suddenly, I shivered with a chill
As if it were autumn instead of spring.

Three days later (oh! what a season to choose!)
Though it was nearly May and tenderness hung
        on the air,
The snows came in a brutal, lashing storm
Tearing down the wires between us so that now

We can no longer reach one another;
Nor bring the food we know the other needs.

NUMBNESS

Dust rising in the sunlight
Streaming through the open window;
The sound of boys' voices
Calling to one another at play—
And I, sitting alone in my room,
Musing on what you said this afternoon.

There was a terrible pressure on my ears
While you were talking, as if it hurt
To hear you say our world had ended.
Then you went on; and I remember
Walking home alone, smiling at people
        and asking them
How they were as if I really meant it.

Somehow I reached the house and climbed
        the stairs
To my room; and I've been sitting here ever
        since,
Watching the dust rising in the sunlight.

THERE IS NO MORE WINE

You feed on memories
Which no longer have substance for you:
Old quarrels, misunderstandings—
While within reaching distance
Are my hands holding a goblet of wine
To revive us.

You turn your head like a child,
Deliberately striking the cup from my hand—
Spilling the wine;
While I stare horrified
At the last of it
Staining my feet.

GREENWICH VILLAGE
1935 - 1937

The damp, unpleasant smell of subway entrances,
descent into the cold tomb of the city and the
flipping of coins at a change booth,
a nickel in the slot
and a downtown train to Sheridan Square.

Walking home through West Fourth to the
    Sixth Avenue L
and spotting overhead the *Hindenburg* en route
to its fiery death; then south into Cornelia,
feeling through the balls of my feet
a sense of adventure in the now-darkened street.

Stopping in Bleecker
for escarole, apples, black olives and cheese;
crusty Italian bread,
garlic,
and a string of purple onions.

Entering the patio through a black iron gate
to a Village apartment for two (more often
    holding two more or twenty)
for tossed salad, a bottle of wine and candlelight;
    and—depending on the mood—
Tchaikovsky, Edna St. Vincent Millay, Etting
    or Leadbelly.

Walking the dog for mutual exercise, and stopping
for a nightcap
at the dimly-lit, smokefilled club on West Third—
its colored orchestra of three men playing off
the pad,
their screeching, hot music
going round and round

The boys with long, curling lashes and wavy hair
who wait on tables and furnish entertainment:
dark boys with shadowy faces,
blond boys with soft tender skin and blue eyes;
their beautiful hands with polished fingernails,
their soft, lovely speech
and delicate trills of laughter;
their hard, wise eyes,
their bold, appraising eyes,
their lonely, bewildered eyes;

Going round and round
the girls sitting at corner tables,
creating atmosphere:
girls with fine, close cropped heads and odd faces,
girls with strong, clean hands
and low, husky voices,
girls with infectious, hearty laughter
and large, free gestures,
girls with futile eyes and empty hands.

The patrons: men and women of shameless
curiosity,
smoking, drinking, staring.
Men with disgusted eyes,
women with frightened eyes;
men with superior eyes,
women with inviting eyes—

The thrill-seekers,
the wiseacres,
the pitiers,
the on-the-makers,
the bored,
the do-gooders,
alcoholics,
psychologists,
the shocked,

All watching with un-understanding eyes
the blond boys, the dark boys of graceful,
languid movements.
All watching with un-understanding eyes
the girls with the brave heads and proud hands.

The music grows hotter and a dancer falls
from exhaustion;
the music grows wilder, louder—drowning
out the
insulting remarks of the self-righteous.

But not before those boys who are waiting
 on tables or singing
and those girls who are seated at tables
have heard.

What in God's name gives you the courage
 to endure this life?

Could it be that
out of all those curious, sneering eyes, once
 in a while
you find eyes that are understanding
 and grateful?
Grateful for momentary recognition
 and the warm,
speechless welcome you give them?

Is *that* your compensation?

THE GAY SPOT

Oh! Self-deceived
Are those pitiables
Who seek anchorage
In these waters.

No Painted Porch
At Stoic Athens,
Nor an
Epicurean Garden

Out of Samos
Is this dim-cornered house
Resting
Darkly beside the bay.

Rather:

A promenade
Where no one walks;
An inverted Elysium
Pointed

To hell
For the lonely experienced
And, alas!
The bewildered young.

A port in the storm
To anyone with silver in his hand,
Change
Being

The coin of blood-red eyes,
Insuppressible
With its wares,
Willing to barter

Commodities—
New or strangely familiar—
For others
Oddly the same.

C'EST PARIS

Paris at night—
Wanton—a woman with dew'd eyes beaming.
Visioned soft white
Of tree-patterned lights, curved waters gleaming.

Champs-Elysées,
Notre Dame and *La Place de la Concorde;*
Black mystic Seine
And silence at the foot of *Sacré Coeur.*

Early bells mark
Dawn's rosy, morning-scented libations.
Mass at *Saint Roche;*
Pungent smell of red and white carnations.

Wine by Pierre;
White walls, *grande dame,* books and a miniature.
Paintings that bear
In themselves their legacy of culture.

Purple pity
Of Versailles: Lovely Austrian with bed
Denied by Louis—
Tinker; and drone about Love's honeyed head.

Match boxes gay
For memory. Hurried taxi traffic.
Darker than day,
Two would hold back Time's incessant toc-tic.

Sun-drenched, incensed
Orléans' stones hallowed because of Jeanne's
    last sigh.
St. Hubert's feast
Horned by red-clad hunters as foxes cry.

Stone-carved Amboise!
Choiseul: Cheese, bread and wine; and, far above
Misty Loire,
Gargoyles peering at astonished new love.

On return from Europe:
October 31, 1961

"Every time I cross the Seine,
*I think of you . . . "**

And remember one October night—
Its Egyptian darkness ablaze
With the lights of the *Pont Neuf*
Flung over the rail

Like stars on shimmering saffron ribbons
Bursting into topaz crosses
As they dropped into
The rippling waters of the Seine.

An Ethiopian lesbian,
The black mystic Seine
Lies with undulating abandon
Across ancient Paris.

With cabalistic fingers
And honeyed tongue,
The river caresses her Left Bank
And her Right—

Renewing with jeweled touch
The youth and beauty, the joy!
She exulted in—centuries ago—
When Paris first lay down beside her.

**From a recent letter from Paris.*

OPEN WOUND

Be not surprised nor hurt,
New Love,
When you touch this heart
Even ever so gently,
That it should quiver in your hand
With remembrance.

FROM THE CROSS

Inspired by the Good Friday Service

Oh! My Love, what have I done to thee?
Or wherein have I brought thee grief?
        Answer me.
Because I led thee out of slavery,
I bear now the cross thou dost lay upon me.

Because I freed thee of thy fears,
I bear now the cross thou dost lay upon me.

What more wouldst thou have me do
        that I have not done?
I opened a new life before thee
And now thou dost open my side
        with indifference.

I went before thee as a column of fire.
I was at thy right hand by day and at thy left.
I followed after thee into the darkness of night
And now thou dost enclose me with shadows.

I quenched thy thirst for clear water
And now thou dost burn my lips with gall.
Oh! My Love, what have I done to thee?
Or wherein have I brought thee grief?
        Answer me.

For thy sake, I smote the winter's Philistines
And now—*in April*—thou dost deliver me
to their camp.

I wrapped thee in a royal robe
And placed a diadem on thy head,
But thou hast stripped me naked
And hast crowned me with thorns.

With a mighty joy, I burnished thy spirit
to gold
And now thou dost hang me from this tree.

Oh! My Love, what have I done to thee?
Or wherein have I brought thee grief?
Answer me.

Answer me?

THAT WHICH YOU HAVE

Her spirit was an outstretched hand,
Brushing your forehead
With its cool touch.

Her spirit was an embrace,
Quieting your impatient, analytical mind
With its warmth—

A gold chalice, a blue Grecian urn
Filled to the brim
With your secret yearning.

Her spirit was dear and charitable,
Giving of itself
To comfort your heart.

Her spirit was wise,
But humbly unaware
How deeply you drank of it.

Spoken and unspoken words
Welded the understanding,
        deep and wonderful,
Between you.

And always, at the thought of her,
You were aware of her friendship
And proud.

It was anticipating
The stimulation of her mind,
The ease of her presence,

That brightened your morrows,
As the glow of the setting sun
Beckons another day.

Death seems cruel and senseless
To those whom it separates,
As if there were an irretrievable loss.

But her hand is still outstretched to you

And she stoops now from Eternity
To tell you that which you had,
You have now forever.

THE GOLDEN RING

What is this dissonant note?
This harsh, inharmonious, inconsistent note?
A rift within the lute,
Out of tune; discordant; denying scope

To the meaning of the sound and sight
Of the carousel we rode,
At once gay and round;
Of the circus horse
We tamed
With soft, unnamed morsels of the night,

What is this I discard?
Looking like a black rose
Trailing bright red ribbon bows
Over the silver plate on my table—
Is it your visitor's card?

I cannot stop to sing or care.
I have lost something.
I am sure it is in the house somewhere,
But I find it neither here nor there.

The golden ring!
What have you done with the golden ring
You won for me at the Fair?
Oh! What have *I* done with the golden ring
You won for me at the Fair?

A SEASON BETWEEN

Now that Autumn's uncertainty
Sears my flesh,
Old loves are intensified;

And new ones—hardly guessed at
When I had but one—
Fill the wine-cask of my being

So I may strengthen the young
Who tramp to my door
For refuge out of a storm;

Or warm the heart
Of an old friend
The first cold night of the coming winter.

I BRING YOU A CHERRY

It is beyond my love
To make you happy,
Unless—like a canary—
Your heart sings of itself.

Yet, like a bird
Eyeing a fruit, your heart
Attributes its joy to every look
Of mine, to every word.

Nonetheless, I do not hesitate
To bring you a cherry in my hand.
You are wise. Aye, full-grown! And
You will know how to checkmate its stone.

I LOVE YOU

Let us sheathe the sword of anger.
No more can we stand its clangor.
The hot, hurting word
In heaven is overheard—

And All Saints' joy one day by our love aglow
By the next is destroyed by All Souls' sorrow.

Our atoning hearts can prevail
To free our imprisoned nightingale
Whose singing—remember?—can so well move
the night
By the unforgettable melody of its nuptial rite.

IRRESOLUTE

Ash stirs easily
With every little breath.
So why stand
There
Then,
In this strong wind,
Not knowing enough
To shield your
Eyes
Tearing now with soot?

Is it because you
Remember soft sounds of
Cloud-spilled rain
Once;
Or—
Better twice still—
Gay, high-jinks laughter
In tree tops
Wild
With wind in sunlight?

LOVE IS JOY

Love is joy!
An almond-bearing rod
Blossoming everlastingly;

The usurper of the heart
Unaffected, unalterable . . .
Ravisher of the innocents

And, forever after,
Utterly fascinating
With its radiance.

It is
aberlard
nijinsky
don quixote

Key-stone, seedling, crown of life—
Precocious and delicate
As April.

Aladdin's lamp . . .
His magic carpet
For exiles from Eden

Down the years,
The centuries drenched in tears,
To the time without end.

BARGAIN IN ZANZIBAR

A work of art, a car, a glove
For your *birthday?*
These things are your due, my Love—
They will not keep you by my side
If you decide
To go away.

FOR LAURA

Dawn prayers for Laura
Stretch on memory's golden string
Across a wide, wide continent
To animate her day's beginning.

Fondly night's blessings
Slide down a silvery moonbeam
That first climbs the snowy Rockies
To keep her safe, to keep safe the dream

She has for her own—
Cherished by her, their grandmother—
For whose happiness (and her own)
She left one ocean for another

With her furniture
And some very precious things—
Like the hat she wore at her son's wedding,
And my music-box angel with pointed wings . . .

For Laura Bond

June 3, 1974

A ROBBER IN CORINTH

Would you kill my spirit? You?
By whom I have been willingly robbed
In this Corinthus
Between heaven and hell?

Would you do this to me,
Whom you have captured
And fastened to the top
Of the fir-tree of your heart,
Bending me to you
With such joy, such ecstasy
And then,
At whim,
Letting me spring up again
Until I die?

NOLLE PROSEQUI

Neither criminal
Nor civil
Was your theft.

I will not press suit.
My heart is
Closed. Finished.

THERE ARE SOME

There are some
With no sense, no knowledge
Of the love that is in a heart:
The hallowed palladium

For neighbor,
For a friend . . . for a foe . . .
For the ill-starred, sorely wounded
By the stroke of the Saber . . .

And for those
With no sense, no knowledge
Of the love that is in a heart . . .
Ay! Who knows the heart? Who knows?

WHAT YOU MEAN TO ME

What are you to me?
Why not ask
What nectar is to the bee?
Or ask
What rudders mean to ships;
Or what a kiss is to the lips?

ARE YOU ADVERSE TO ME? OR AVERSE TO ME?

Even now, we spoke
Our usual goodnight
On the telephone
And all our antipathy
Was cloaked for the night.

But you alone,
With me alone,
Must surely agree:
You are either adverse to me
Or you are averse to me.

I do not know
If you have set your face
Against me;
Or if my being
Goes against your grain.

Nor can I ascertain
What it is that owes
Our love its life.

It lives!
Of this, there is no doubt.
But the strife between us
Is about to do me in
Because I cannot tell
If adverse you've been
Or—come hell
Or high water—
Averse.

GRAPES OF PINK WAX

Grapes of pink wax
are not all that ugly
as you might think—
just sighting the words
grapes of pink wax—
until they turn out to be

Waxed
grapes of wrath,
belying the laughter
that tickled me
that night
I found them
on my pillow
after seeing you off;

Belying
the laughter that rang
through the phone
when you sang to me
that old song
from some far off place,
from way off in
Europe or Asia or Africa
or wherever you'd gone.

And I told you what a sly
devil you were to remind me,
in that sly way, of
your absence.

You said then
that you did want them back—
that they were a centerpiece
or something,
something to set off
a black table cloth
or something.

But all these years
I neglected to return them
for the simple reason
that everytime I opened
the drawer I'd put them in
for safekeeping
that silly grin would
spread over my face

And because I remembered then
how stiff I'd been with cold
when we first met
and you were so warm and
round;

And the thick wet fog
that quickly set in,
enveloping me
from the ground up
so I could not see ahead,
not even my hand
in front of my face.

And I neglected to return them,
as I said,
because whenever I opened
that drawer where I'd put them
for safekeeping,
I'd laugh again,
remembering the night
I turned down my bed
and discovered them
on my pillow
while you were still
over the Atlantic
or the Pacific
or the Indian
or whatever ocean.

Hurray! (You'd never guess
        their age.)
for the make-believe grapes!

they have survived
beautifully,
pinked and waxed.

But not the real ones
you gave to me and
I gave to you
so generously:
the real grapes
of such a wide variety,
we could *eat*
and be filled
and there'd be seven baskets
left over.

They stand empty now.

But not my bed!
grape seeds are spread
over my sheets
like bread crumbs
dropped by someone eating
carelessly
in bed.

And I'm so un-
comfortable sleeping.

Well, here's your centerpiece.

A SINGLE YELLOW ROSE

She came to my door—
Love's lovely spendthrift—
Bearing a gift:
A single yellow rose.

"We will not be lovers,"
I said, last night.
(Although there is no other to underwrite
My joys, my woes.)

The house, emptied now,
Screamed its silence.
Contested my self-defense.
I won! At four this morning,

I went to bed
And slept and slept and slept . . .
Alone, at last, and free! *Except*
There was no warning

That, twelve hours later,
My hands would fly against love's hurt—
I would become sea-girt
And awash with pain.

I cried then
For my love . . .

Nor knew whereof
Came the rain

That chilled me thru and thru;
Nor the lightning—sharp, jagged, white—
That knifed my eyes,
Leaving me uninhabited.

"Don't call me," she had warned.
"Don't call me!"
Don't call me—
Love's rejection rabbeted.

"I NEED YOU!"

She came then to my door
Her smile lost, adrift . . .
Bearing a gift:
A single yellow rose

From her garden.
Not a bramble rose—a *rose,*
A single yellow rose
From her garden.

SOME THERE ARE
WHO LIVE THE LORD'S LAST PASSOVER

Come!
Take up your cross
And follow
Me!

All of you who are abandoned,
Are betrayed by lover, spouse, or kin, or friend:
Stay your heart! Take up your cross
And follow Him.

Follow Him to the Upper Room
Where His friends drink wine
As if tomorrow were not doomed,
And sing a song yet unheard in Eire.

Follow Him to the Upper Room
Where one He called His trusted friend
Dips his bread in the same dish with Him:
O privileged act so long familiar,

And now so full of foreboding!

Follow Him later this night when—
Backed by spears that pierce the moon—
Judas dares to sign Him,
Dares to wound Him with a kiss.

Do you know—
You who are betrayed,
Abandoned—that your dismay
Is Christ's? That you are one with Christ?

And oh!
That—soon—you will rise again?

WE REAP WHAT WE SOW

There are three sides
To every story.
You know yours,
And I know mine.
The truth lies in between.

But this you can't deny:
You abandoned me.
I
Did not abandon you.

Now, five long years
After you left me
(Add to them the drought
Of seven cleft by secrecy),
You have chosen
To revive your frozen love,
To sound the same promises
You did not keep
The first bleak time around.

I succumbed anew last season—
Don't ask me why—
To the softest voice I ever knew.

Oh, yes! The same soft voice
That gave, then took away,
Your love; and now, for a reason
Still unspoken,
You want to give it back again.
I never could read you,
Even in Braille.

Moreover,
After all these years,
I still don't know
Your mother's name
Or where she lies buried.
Or if you have a sister
Or a brother.

My dear, you claim you love me?

This has become a dreary tale.
Quickly now, I'll make
An end of it.

We reap what we sow.

And so,
I say

Goodbye.

WHEN DREAMS EXPLODE IN SMOKE

Your song, your laughter, your impeccable
street manners
Will never offset, for me,
Your miserable insistence on
Both your righteousness and your rightness.

Getting your own way, no matter the cost,
May be acceptable to others,
But never to me; unless first
You hear me out.

I told you before—
At the very least,
Give me my birthright:
A chance to express myself,

No matter how wrong I may be
Or you may think I am.
But at the very least, give me a chance.
But you won't and don't.

What are you afraid of?

This is a country
Dedicated to free expression
Without arrest
Or jail, or even inhibition,

Or private oppression such
As I've experienced from you
Without recourse.
I am a free spirit, American besides.

If our mutual friends
Abandon me, it is best for me that I'll know
They never were friends
Of mine.

But if I must sacrifice
Those I've learned to love
That's okay too, though a disappointment;
Not as great for sure,

But close nonetheless to mine in you.

I've been praying to God for us:
For our health, our house, our future dreams.
And I never dreamed He'd allow a quarrel
In which I'd find His answer.

THAT WHICH YOU MADE, YOU KNOW

We know that You, who made us, know us.
Even among men,
Which of them does not know
What he builds and mends with his own hands;
What he alone intends in his mind?

Risking rebellion and unbelief,
You endure reproach
By not granting
Vociferant whims; but brief, adjure
Your children's approach to the blessed fief.

You have provided for us the love
Of a family;
The ampullae
That hold the wine and water of life:
Work and play, mind and spirit. Friendship.

For that which You made, You know.

We trust that Your most dangerous gift—
Our will's delight,
Prized liberty—
Will be used aright, with grace, by us;
That we do not abase Your favors.

For this is the source of suffering
In the innocent
Whose sacrament
Of life is inbred in its chalice;
Betrayed, without malice aforethought.

Guiltless to the last, their hurt becomes
Their encrusted ankh—
For even here,
You outflank their pain with Your Christus,
His undeserved bier, His mother's cross.

For that which You made, You know.

CELEBRATION FOR JUDY

We shall not weep for you, dear Judy.
At the height of your beauty,
On the wings of the wind you flew.
We shall not weep for you.

Nor shall we essay
Sad, disillusioned Millay,
Who cried, being disinclined,
*I am not resigned.**

Weep? No. No. No!
Tears are not in this folio.
Why weep? You left priceless gems, and trinkets
Of laughter in our pockets.

You are with God.
Your heart, an Aaron's rod,
Struck love from every rock.
And your hand was soft as the softest glove.

* * * * *

Don't embarrass me, she said,
My record's still unread.
Then in jest (ne'er given to boasting):
He's way behind in His posting!

Merrily her waggish prattle swung upon a star.
From afar
We saw it winking,
Setting all of heaven twinkling.

We laughed with the whole wide sky!
When, suddenly, we cried.
We knew not why.
(Oh, but we do! We do!)

To Celie, with memories of Judy
May 15, 1978

*From *Dirge Without Music*
by Edna St. Vincent Millay

GOLDEN WERE HER HANDS

As she moved carefully
Through the forest
All her own,
Here and there
From treetops—
Where it shone like a coif
Under a nun's veil—
Without vows,
Sunlight slithered to the ground
Like a golden snake
And lay coiled,
On her forest bed,
Its waving, dancing head
Awakening April in her heart.

One day—unexpectedly and quite unafraid—
A bluebird flew into her quiet hands.
And stayed . . .
And low, blurry notes—
Canterbury's bell also—
Were heard across the land,

Blessed was the time they passed
In meadow grass
Smelling of sunshine
And the smoking wick
Of candleberry.

For their proving had begun.

Quickly then,
On one awe-struck day,
They saw a mountain—
Made of amethyst—
Moving toward them.

They never noticed it was wearing
A cockatrice in its hair . . .

Soon—
Much too soon—
When the May apple was in bloom,
The sun was eclipsed.

Blue wings were flying by,
Flying away.

And night fell
Where once a light had shone.

* * * * *

When next the May apple bloomed,
She was herself entombed.

Her hands, a golden cup become,
Holding forever
The sacred crumbs
Of a maximum memory . . .
Of a holy memory . . .

In memory of
Cecilia Weinschenk
May 24, 1979

LOVE'S HOMECOMING

My heart winged to the sky
When your plane flew wide and high
Out of the fog over London.

With dips and turns, sure and quick,
It heads for the Atlantic
To catch the yellow dawn.

Candlelight and wine
And three red roses—sign
Of love so true—wait for you.

But first, my arms
Like flying gendarmes
Will swoop upon you, catch you

And hold you fast
In the embrace forecast
By our separation.

My body—like clematis—
Will twist and cling to yours,
My kiss will tell you

You are home . . .

*. . . sans everything**

Long before you were released
From this limbus of hell,
The music of your womanhood
Diminished in tempo and decibel
As its semiquavers—
Barely whispering now—fell from a staff
No longer strong enough to hold them.

Helplessly we witnessed
These calando days and listened
To the hollow hooting of the owl
Standing watch at the bivouack
Where Death planned his attack.

He flaked your movements
Throughout the country
Of which you were a native;
He silenced your song
For the people to whom
You belonged.

You became an anchorite
Not from religious light.
And long before the fury of the battle,
We sensed an empty space about you—

Something was out of place
In your dear face:
You were withdrawn—
You left us bereft before you left.

Oh, hear the anguished cry
Of the one who helped you weather
A lifetime. It pierces God's heart—
Does it not yours?
Her tears run down your cheeks
As plaintively she sighs,

Oh, remember me? Remember me?

Nor did she realize that the Lord was most kind
To blind your inner sight.
He knew you would have been disinclined
To go Home peacefully had you known
You were leaving her behind.

In memory of
Evalyn Schaller
January 11, 1990

*Shakespeare's *As You Like It*

THE IRONY OF DREAMS

There is a hamlet on the Island—
Bearing an Indian name—
Where so easily did I live with you,
Making love to you was like a snowflake
Fallen straight from God, and pure . . .

So judged my conscience
That—always prickly—
Found sleep with you peaceful—
Painless—like a toothache
Overcome by Novocain.

Truly this love
Was a gift from God . . .
Yet God seems jealous
Of His own gifts—
There is no giving them
Without their being taxed
With pain and suffering:
You had a heart attack.

And I left our bed
To save your strength.
Not like lovers—
As everyone thought—

But like sisters
We lived those years.
And no one knew the difference.

Nor could what we did
For the house and for each other
Be measured against one another.
It was—as you said
Of the sweaters you knitted for me—
A labor of love.

And oh! that feeling
Of being at home—
So intense then,
So intense in this dream
That came to my dozing.

I was reaching for the phone
When I woke up—
To tell you
I'll buy back the old house—
We'll live together again . . .

Forgetting that I had just gotten word
That you are dying—
That, even now, you may be dead . . .

Forgetting that dreams are Lazarus
Returned from the grave
With the odor of spice about him—
That waking is Lazarus from head to toes
Still wrapped in his burial-clothes . . .

Forgetting that—silvery-white
And fettered by the irons
Of our golden days—we now lie
Head to the Wind,
Unable to turn either way . . .

Forgetting that nothing *ever*
Can be the same again . . .

FRIENDSHIP

My balloon skims the air as easily
And notedly as, without moving a limb,
A swimmer with flair floats on water.

All the world looks up to see
My hard-run balloon shining in the sky—
Obliged as the moon to an absentee sun.

No stop, I thought, to its flight when suddenly,
Without warning, it lands atop a tree. Pops!
        Bursts!
Even before noon, and within sight of the loons

Who notice not, in the end,
That ever-important string
Safely ringed in the hand of a friend.

MY SOLE GIFT

Ah, Achates!
Do not tease me
With your thirsty heart,
That copious, cordate cup
Designed by God
To be filled up
With the wine
Of unspoiled
Honeyed nights,
And sighted days
Anointed with oil.

Yes! I could love you that way,
Yet because I am tied to Him,
I must love you in another way.
Nor would I have you cry again.

O friend unique,
Whose loyalty is precious to me,
Although you cannot forget
How your Troy was destroyed,
I can yet give you joy
With the sole gift left to me:

Uncurséd,
Crystal-clear water
To pour into
Your extraordinary amphora
To slake its Greek and ancient thirst.

For Barbara Tervo

ONCE IN A COOL, GREEN WOOD

Once I walked alone
In a cool, green wood
And pulled its peace around me
Like a warm and hooded Capuchin.

Indeed! Autumn-chilled, Silvanus
Had started to shiver
As Apollo regaled him
With his breezy laughter

And dripped his mirth
Like orange pips
All over the earth,
All over the trees.

And I stopped to see
What happens to leaves
Edged in chalk and purple,
In brown and red and yellow.

Suddenly, with a beguiling flutter,
A bird flew across my eyes,
Uttering a song as sweet,
As wild as I have ever heard.

Then winging *a balletto*,
She flew high through that elfin light,
Then down with stilled feathers
Blue, oh! bluer than blue.

So prettily she danced
Above me and below;
In the air; near the ground:
Around me, and above.

Eccentric were our circles,
While I kept spinning, turning,
Searching everywhere
For my darting bird.

Then all at once
—Hush! O Forest!—
I found her there before me:
Perched, *en pointe*, upon a fern,

And waiting for me.

REJUVENESCENCE

There were two windows in the front
Of the old house
That, in autumn, caught fire
From the setting sun.
And you'd think the house ablaze.

But the house had been abandoned.

The front door—still good—hid from the curious
The falling plaster,
The creaking boards;
Cobwebs in odd corners, but mostly
Circling the ceiling.

The house, you see, had been abandoned.

There was a grapevine
Whose grapes had shriveled
For lack of care;
An old stone well,
Long since gone dry.

And in the front yard, in spring,
A cherry tree gloried whitely—
Then dripped red, next season,
When its fruit, half-eaten by winged wastrels,
Fell to the ground to rot.

Men and women, passing by,
Longed to pick the cherries.
But standing behind a stone wall,
The tree was very private.
Besides, they feared the house was haunted.

It had been, as I said, abandoned.

Then, one day, behold!
A woman stood before the stone wall,
Intrigued at how and why
The sun—so *many million* miles away—
Had chosen *those* two front windows
To set ablaze
When everything else around
Remained in shadow.

She loved mystery, and abandoned-poetry.

She breached the wall.
She walked tentatively to the house
And pushed open the door.
It was easy.
The house was helpless . . .

It had been abandoned, as I said.

She saw, then, what it must have been
Before the plaster crumbled,
The floor boards crunched;
And what the spiders had stuffed
In their pockets.

One song—
Sung in a lilting Celtic voice—
Bought the house for her.
It was only a token.
But the house
Remembers the song . . .

As if in a movie run backward,
Its walls donned again their white coats.
Floorboards became quiet, listening for her.
And spiders were trapped in their own webs
By her Irish laughter.

Some magic rod
She held
Struck water, filling the droughty well.
And sap rose—tipsily—
In the ancient vine.

At last,
She came to the tree
And plucked a single cherry. Tasted.
Then filled her mouth with them—
So sweet were they to her tongue . . .

She lay down, then,
Under the tree
And saw
The *sky*
Through its branches.

They are good for each other:
The woman and the old house
Whose two front windows
Blaze now at *all* seasons—
From within.

Her hair, you see, *is the color of the sun.*

RENOIR WOMAN

France should have been your home.
At least *Armorica*—
Seaside refuge become Brittany (after Rome)
For Celts fleeing Anglo-Saxon phobia.

With Venus in mind, Renoir
Would have painted you—
A statuesque-limbed *Matrona*
Pulling up blue stockings

At the edge of the sea.

Defenceless breasts—
Shaped by ravaging waves—
Startling white, roundest, twin stones
Revenge themselves by spilling purple wine.

Massive, fiery pillars
Guard—between them—your shadowy,
        coral strait.
Roguish, circular, scooped-out hollows
Recreate your back for playing in the sand.

Sea spray is your hair,
Celtic-gold in the sun.
Your navel is a snare for oblivion
In the midst of your belly.

Deep in your sea-colored eyes
Swims the primeval mystery of the waters—
Moving restlessly, complying with the moon.
Endlessly reaching for it. Aswoon.

A TIME OF JOY

Nature, reflecting
God's face,
Is perfumed forever with
The primeval breath He
Exhaled: Sustenance
For man. Booty from Eden.
Emmanuel for us
Who heed such transcendent
Grace, which engrails our hearts
Twice over when
He bedecks them with
A friend.

THERE BEING TIMES WHEN . . .

Now that I am seventy-five
With some taste buds still alive,
With great longing, I often long
For the first taste of apple wine
That, at the age of five or three,
Seduced me under the new-leafed tree.

And I yearn for childhood's laughter—
Those uncontrollable giggles—
Over what I can't remember;
Over nothing, my mother
Discovered, except that her child
Was enamored of apple wine.

Even now,
I dream of my first taste of it
And wake up laughing a fit,
Catching my breath in endless gasps
The way I used to as a kid;

Yet now
More like a child holding its breath
While it cries.

FOR THIS, THERE IS NO NAME

I should be prepared
(But I never am)
For this sudden push
Into a mad, mad sea
Where my lungs lack air.
And my eyes,
Bottled up in liquid glass,
Cannot see
What it is
That stirred up
The mud from the bottom.

With my head above,
There is joy
In the water.
And its buoyancy—
Deporting all my weight—
Holds me up,
Supports me like a toy balloon.

Pooled water, lined with laughter—
Cooling me.
Refreshing me.
Shining with a sun
All its own; with joy—

Spoiled, so soon,
By this untimely push;
Roiled water
Blinding me more than I am blind.

I am there at the bottom.
I cannot see.
I cannot see.
I cannot breathe.

Oh! Reach me down, my Love!
Reach your hand,
Long overdue,
Or I shall surely drown.

A FRAGRANCE ESCAPED FROM HEAVEN

Thrice sweet was Heaven made
With the fragrance of His Love
Before creation knew
A Paradise; so too,
Earth became fragrant,
Thrice sweet,
When He flamed our love.

A DAY AND A NIGHT IN A SPECIAL SEA

Thighs and legs, long devoted to the sun,
Glisten darkly under his Southern brush;
Brown spanker, parted in two, propels you
To my side, anchored in this blue and tiny sea.
"Swim!" you say, exhort! "or sail your river-boat."

* * * * *

Moonbeams break: you rise from the sea's
embrace.
Ah! Venus-crafted, gold-centered daisy
Floating free, with fireflies skimming ahead
On water-wings. Aphrodite, Dionysus
Cavort: drink pink wine from living conches'
shells.

WHERE ARE YOU, MY LOVE?

Once, as starlight,
Our rapture was scintillating and gay
Yesternight—oh, yesternight!
In lovely Mandalay.

When tenderness held the night,
Our love—in its secret way—
Filled with laughter because the world came right
Yesterday—oh, yesterday!

KM in Carrollton, Georgia

1984

at 76

Part III

DAWN

(Apperceiving the Spiritual Path)

To the Glory of God

BORN AGAIN

I thought it a gay troubadour
Who left his footmark on my path
As I went a-larking
Playing my birth-day fife.

Flawed was my sight
All lifelong
Until that sleepless night
Rapturous, even then, with a siren song

When Thompson's Hound,*
Confounding my every step, any time,
any place,
Caught up with me, at last.
And naught would do, except I look
into His Face.

Nor saw I ever such a beauteous face.
All those aureate things we mortals love
Are but metaphors for parts of the whole
Concealed, contained, and completed
in that Face:

The turbulent breaks of the trackless sea,
The peaceful wonder of woodland lakes.
The light of a Capulet moon
Silhouetting an ebony tree.

Red flames burning an autumn sky
At eventide,
A blue wing
Clinging to a branch.

Mountains, not outdone in grandeur,
With cherubim stretching the sun
Just above their rim.
Curious aurora lighting frozen lamps.

Empyreal stars
Sparkling in the black of night.
The taste of new-blown snow.
The freshness alone, the greening also,
of rain.

Grain leaning in the field
Feeding the elemental hunger of man.
Potatoes, corn, greens and tomatoes
Sustaining him for those precious hours,
Gentle and joyful with new-sprung flowers.

The human desire for love.
The white foxglove-innocence of babes;
Of wild beasts, fishes,
and feathered artistes.

The golden dreams of women.
The regimes of men.
Their work, their strivings.
Their play. Their strife.

Democracies.
History and philosophy.
Technocracies.
Science. The arts. Theology.

All these are parts
Of the whole concealed,
Contained, and completed
In that Face.

Alas! These, too:

The burden
Of men's erstwhile self-dooming sin
Assumed by the Christ upon His Cross.
Aye! The reproof in those Eyes!
        O! The sorrow

Over man's continuous running, still,
After evil. Over his willing embrace
Of debasing corruption,
The disgrace, the degradation of his soul.

All this—
The rejection by His creatures.
Their indifference, the vomitory of God.
        Of the Lord!
Whose featured gifts reflect His glory—
        all this

Is in that Face
That transcends in grace and beauty
All other love,
All other loveliness.

My soul soars! Would race to heaven
Since I saw His Face, one night.
My heart, uncongealed at last,
Is burned out by His igniting grace.
        And healed.

For born-again
Jimmy Carter
on his inauguration as the
thirty-ninth President
of the United States
January 20, 1977.

*The symbol of the Lord Jesus Christ,
as envisioned by Francis Thompson
in his poem
The Hound of Heaven

JOHN XXIII

The rock of Faith: Peter
Not only, but also
John, the Beloved—
The lover.

ROMA
October 25, 1961

AN ECUMENICAL PROTEST

Who was careless
With this candle?
Who left soundless
Our vesper-bell?

PORTRAIT OF A NUN

She is fascinated by many things:
Antiques and precious stones,
Fine linens and silver bowls;
Satins in the latest fashions
And lovely, crazy hats.

Poverty, thank you for freeing my soul.

Babies, little girls and redhaired boys.
The sacrifice of parents for their children;
And the love that
Binds them together.

Chastity, thank you for the beauty of God
in all.

Wild roses; the ballet; and walking in the rain.
The first crocus; poetry and the arts;
Silence of falling leaves; the old; the dreams
of the young,
And all things full of courage and independence.

Obedience, thank you for teaching me
God's will.

All these things,
And much more in the secret of her heart,
She gives with sparkling joy—
With *gaieté de coeur*—to God, her love.

And He gives back to her:

The poor

Who are rich in her presence;

The sick

Who leave their pain in her hands;

The ignorant

Whose eyes she opens to life and to God.

Thank you for these gifts, my Lord,
And for Your love.
Time is swift, my Lord!
Give me Thy grace;
Help me to persevere.
Have Mercy. Oh!
My Jesus, mercy!

For Sister M. Rose de Lima Moran, R.S.M.

BENEDICTION AT LADYROCK

Before She was made,
This tremendous boulder was created
And set there carefully with His own hands:
An altar awaiting Her image.

To the Indians—
Although She was their Mother unknown—
Her Rock was already their trusted shield,
Their secure refuge from enemies.

Who knows when the saint
Jogues, envisioning this sanctuary,
Blessed this Rock on his tortured path to death?
Or if, once, it was his altar stone?

Now, white clouds vest Him
While the wind burns the incense of His breath . . .
And an acolyte sky spreads its blue cope
In hèr honor—on Mary's morning.

A benediction
For us, God sanctifies this sacred spot
With His golden monstrance shining atop
A distant mountain. Dawn-tipped birches

In candelabra
Flame before the sacrament of nature
While the morning star quietly attests
The presence of Nature's holy God.

Intoxicated
With the fragrance of His breath lingering
In the sweet air, songbirds gather to chant
Prime, the first of the Little Hours;

While pine-bough hyssops,
This golden day, glisten still with soft rain
Which blessed—during nocturnal Asperges—
This earth, reverent now; and aware

Of Mary conceived without sin.

Feast of the Assumption
At LADYROCK
Chestertown, New York

CHRISTMAS COMES *EVERY YEAR* TO AN UNHAPPY WORLD

The world could be the Child tonight,
Wrapped in swaddling clothes of snow—
A white-wooled Israelite,
God's glory to those who know.

Be still, O man!
Let no battle cry frighten childlike sleep
Of gut-torn soldiers,
Of comrades-in-arms who sigh

For peace,
And damn the death watch—
In Israel and Vietnam—
As a bloody botch

That keeps them far from
Home-town streets
Unmarked, as yet, by the blasted bomb;
Far from their loves, from all that life completes.

So keen—*any* Christmas—their remembrance,
It could be their faltering
Were not their hoped-for deliverance
From doomsday incised by their slaughtering.

Indeed, the world could be the Child tonight,
Bloodied now from the wounds of its birth,
But that it is unwashed, uncared for still, by those
who would indict
God for a dead star, and peace remiss on earth.

STAR-CROSSED

Betrayed is John, that gentle priest;
Betrayed—his love, his hope—
By a world overpoliced,
Rebellious, blindly agrope . . .
Its obedience now sworn to a horoscope.

For John Paul I

URBI ET ORBI
(To the City and to the World)

From the east, a White Flame
Streaks across the darkened sky:
Uncurled lightning eerily exposing
Maimed, blood-stained corners
Of a fearsome, noisy world . . .
Frame,

With arms stretched wide,
And shadow of his Master's cross
Against the rising curtain of morning,
He comes to our shores—
Black man and brown and yellow
To bless and draw gently to his side.

And to bless the white man,
Flouted and frustrated by the Devil,
Now that this penitent would purge himself
Of his slowly awakened guilt
Charged to him by God in His voice—
The Asian and the African.

Ariel of Peace,
Paul arrives—expectant and unafraid—
This very day his Church is gladdened
By remembrance of love-filled Francis—

To plead with him for his children everywhere
Of every quarrel and creed and shade:

"Lord, make me an instrument of Thy peace."

Dedicated to
His Holiness, Pope Paul VI

In commemoration of the first
papal visit in history to America;
and Pope Paul's appeal to the
United Nations in the cause of peace.

October 4, 1965
Feast of St. Francis of Assisi

A ROSARY FALLS IN SURPRISE

Gold-tipped flames
Consumed her heart
As—
Expectant of another sunrise
And a silver-toned mass bell—
She discovered
Faint, stray moonbeams
Quivering with music . . .
The rosary in her hands,
A garland of black roses
On the walls of her cell.

Her last Aves then
Became a *laudate* song
Pure and strong
From her unpretentious heart.
Her last astonishment:
The feel of Mary's hand in hers.

Now comes the gentle wind of her spirit
Reviving us—still puffed up—
To His willingness to be conquered
By unobtrusive souls

Who, rich in self-knowledge,
Are humble all life long
Before the wonder of His love.

For my friend
Sister Mary Anita, O.P.

ANNIVERSARY MASS FOR MY MOTHER

She was the chalice
Filled with the wine
That became my blood;

The ciborium
Laden with the bread
That became my body.

One day, God spilled the wine . . .
And the bread has been scattered
On the fields these many years.

Ever hungry,
This child, this day,
Would gather up the crumbs.

A BENEDICTINE MONK ON A GEORGIA BATTLEFIELD

A Saga*

How soft were the gutteral sounds
Come forth from a Ratisbon throat.
Gentle, yet strong like none other,
Was the Bavarian accent
Bent over wounded men
Found bleeding on this battlefield . . .

Men—who did not know
They entered a Stygian boat
When they went to war—
Feeling a strange confusion
And pleading with their chaplain
Father, am I going to die?

He did not lie.
With right hand raised
In absolution, he replied:
Come, close your eyes, my son,
And rest. A little sleep
And you will see
Truly you are alive.

So too are the defiant dead
Outstaring Apollo's glaring eye.
His was the first to give in
When he dropped below the trees
At Jonesborough—defeated that day,
As were they in a battle
They could not win.

What more was there to lose?
They had already lost
What could not be spared . . .
The sole remaining rail—
With Macon and Atlanta aboard—
The artery to the deeper South
Cut with a *terrible swift sword.*

These were the brave dead
To whom the monk belonged—
The Bloody Tenth—
Sweet yield of Tennessee . . .
Strewn across the cratered field
Like Holy Bread
Desecrated.

O Sorry Story!
O Glorious Song!
Now intoned
By this humble poem . . .

What the gods demanded more
On that fated day—
The last of August
Eighteen sixty-four—
Caved in the eyes
Passing by . . .

Kentucky, under orders,
Falling to the rear
With the grim-faced survivors
Of her Orphan Brigade.

Its General Joseph Lewis—
Brigadier—
Would tell what he saw—
Sworn genesis
Of a tale to remember
Forevermore.

And this is what he saw . . .
The Chaplain of the Tenth
Kneeling beside his dying colonel,
Found by the priest
On that harried field
And carried to the rear.

This is what the colonel—
William Grace—
Would say that day,
Just before he died,
And how his soul's distress
Had urged him to confess.

O Stricken Soldier!
So anxious to be shriven
Of those warrior-sins
Common to all
Who go to war.

And this is what the general saw:
The priest's hand raised
In absolution . . .
And then, he said,
At once he heard
A roar above his head—
A demon missile,
One of hundreds
Out of that Federal hell—
Cynical, unnecessary—
Strafing with satanic fury
Troops already wounded by defeat.

When next he looked,
Lewis was appalled—
Shaken to his very core
By the curdling sight
Right before his eyes—
The chaplain's headless body
Slumped down upon
His numbed and helpless colonel.

O Purple Wood of Calvary!
The head—anointed—blown off . . .

Ultimate—furious!—
Was the revenge evinced
By an ugly henchman
Of the Evil Prince,
Jealous of the *Te Absolvo*
That robbed him of a soul.

* * * * *

The litter bearers,
Out that night
To retrieve their honored dead,
Never found the Benedictine's head . . .

Into myriad splinters split,
Blown into splotches of blood
Along with that profound look
In those gentle, dove-like eyes—
Eyes mistaken for globs of spit
Twisted into blood-stained scuff
By horses' mindless hooves,
By unsuspecting troops.

* * * * *

Apostolic was the number of years
Since the Catholic son of Ratisbon
Knelt before the Abbot of Latrobe
And solemnly vowed
For the rest of his days
To follow Saint Benedict
In the way he labored,
In the way he prayed.

And within these years was held
The octave since the bishop,
Laying hands upon his head,
Brought forth a priest
Whose heart to God
Was the Hour of Lauds,
Chanting praises to its Lord.

Laudate Dominum was emblazoned
On the candelabrum of his soul,
With new flames sprung
Like Pentecostal tongues.

Into the Vineyard he quickly ran—
Hard, but carefully did he run—
Carrying before him,
In the candlestick
Of his privileged hands,
The Light of Christ
To shed on far corners
Deprived of the Son.

* * * * *

When called to Nashville,
Father Emmeran Bliemel—
Soon caught up in war—
To its very drouth, gave his heart
To the cause of the South.

Now was his city—occupied—
Stripped naked of its
Native trusting ways
By a dictatorship,
Whose magnified and secret eye
Searched for treason everywhere—

In house and church,
In charnel house and pleasure-house,
In amoebic alleyways.

Stalked to a corner there,
The Benedictine was caught—
On his person were shown
Four ounces of morphine,
Some snuff, and a comb.

Arrested, then, for treason,
He was taken to the Union General
Before whom, the monk—
Vowed to poverty, and plainly
Equivocal, claimed the property
Seized was *an investment . . .*
Quote *for the Confederacy,*
Reserved in his heart
For the judgment of God.

The pastor of Assumption Church
Thought it no sin
To smuggle medicine
To men he called his own,
Nor such things
As some snuff and a comb,
Nor to speak out
In defense of the South.

For on this, the day
Of his first arrest,
Had he not made
That incredible statement—
Unrequired, yet volunteered—
By a conscience
That knew no fear?

The South—
So it reads in the report—
Is deprived of its rights.
Its rebellion is justified.
And signed it in black and white?

It was no surprise, then,
That he was arrested a second time—
Accused of authoring
Seditious writing
Published in the North.

Only by the grace of God
Was the prisoner twice released—
The Union General had a brother
Who was the Father's brother-priest.

O Unhappy Benedictine!
Free, and yet not free . . .
A Nazarene denied by Peter
To heal a bleeding battlefield—

Who even as he bore this cross
Must now witness the crucifixion
Of his church.

The priest's grief was as wild
As any father's losing a child.
Who can describe it?
Only his eyes could speak aloud
Those thin white words
Of his bereavement.

Yet God gives again—
In the midst of a depression
So deep he seemed asleep,
The bishop's permission arrived
To revivify his heart.

He could join his men!
He was Chaplain of the Tenth!

* * * * *

Quickly, then, on horseback,
The monk ventured forth—
Equipped with his knapsack
Filled with holy tools:
His chalice and his missal
And the Sacred Book of the Lord.

Armed with unshelled courage
And credentials from his bishop,
He wound a tortuous course
Through enemy lines, and around
And about Union patrols
Who—with peril—maligned
His journey's endless days.

Nor no less were the nights blighted . . .
Sounding with the terrified bark
Of unnerved sentries—alone
And gripped by fear
Of the unknown dark.

At long last, safe and unharmed,
He rode into the Southern camp,
Where the air was instantly split
By its gentlemen-at-arms,
Who shouted with the unbounded joy
Of summer-camp boys
At first sight of someone from home.

* * * * *

There was intimate talk
That night, as one by one,
They entered the tent of their friend—
Their *priest!*—and walked away,
One by one, in peace.

* * * * *

Lo! The morning come
With its rising sun
Unfurling banners—
Pale gold—
Across those early skies
And touching with his lighted taper
Each small drop of dew
That lay upon the grass—
Now a cathedral floor become
For the priest to walk upon—
A fitting passage inlaid with jewels
For the servant of the King
Treading his way toward a canopy
Of trees—nature's *baldacchino*
Of silken leaves, brocaded in
The morning's golden threads.

Under such glory
Stood the altar
Made by the men
From the wood
Of a fallen tree.

In their sight,
The rough-hewn boards
Covered with a cloth
Shone like an altar
Of Italian marble.

And to the thankful priest,
Spreading the gifts upon it,
The altar was as beautiful
As the one in Ratisbon.

Deep was his reverence
As he bent over and kissed it
Before descending to the foot
Of the hill on which it stood.

In nomine Patris, et Filii,
Et Spiritus Sancti. Amen.
Intoned the monk . . .

Thus began the ritual of Love
Borne by the memory
In the blood of centuries
Since that last, never-
To-be-forgotten, Supper.

Came, then, that solemn moment
When, for all the men to see,
The priest raised the gifts
He had brought for them:

A Cup and a Saucer
From their Mother's Table,
And a loaf of Bread
Now being broken
By the Father
To feed his family.

O Divine Morsel!
How sweet is thy taste
Of Home . . .

* * * * *

Indeed, an *Alter Christus*
Was this priest
From across the sea,
From the North and East,
And come to the South . . .

Never to gauge the height
Nor depth of love—
But to give, like Christ,
His young life
In a bloody sacrifice.

Dedicated to the
Father Emmeran Bliemel
Fourth Degree Assembly
Knights of Columbus
Jonesboro, Georgia

*Inspired by
Valiant Chaplain
of the Bloody Tenth
by Peter J. Meaney, O.S.B.

THE JEWS

Hold them dear
For their sakes not only,
But for what they were,
And are, and hope to be:

For bearing
Heroically
Their mystical roles
In history—

Dry-nurse to the human race;
Burnt-offering of the past,
Present and future,
Periodically purging the world of evil;

The patient waiter on Providence.

Hold them dear
For these things
Not only,

But also
Because Mary, His Mother,
Was the Lily of their patriarchal land;
The Cedar of Lebanon

Who, by her acceptance, her *Fiat!*
Endowed forever
The blood in their veins
With the subconscious remembrance

Of Christ, *their Brother.*

CELEBRATE THE CHRIST

Rest blest and merry, Ladies and Gentlemen!
And blest and merrier be your Children, who
Trace your love, your beauty and your grace
In the Gothic windows of your space.
Festoon your halls! Celebrate the Christ!
Yes! Celebrate! Negate not His highest call:

To render justice to all. To all
Humanity. To women. For fairest justice aspires
to what
Eternity solely requires. From this virtue,

Every virtue flows save mercy.
Recall, O Man! God's justice outraged at Eden's
groan.
And the debt yet unpaid the Woman through
whom His Mercy shone.

Not on men alone! Ah! Christ's Equality!
O Divine Example! Light the brightest lamp
When men, at last, amend their Law according,
Lord, to Thee.

DEFRAUD NOT THE WIDOW OF HER SORROW

O Widow! You are alone,
Yet not alone.
See! How close you are to Me!—

To Me, God's only Son begot,
The Son who learned
Man's common lot.

My wounds sting afresh
To your tears—so linked
Is my Flesh to their salt.

Every nightfall
My nailéd Feet stalk
The sound of his steps

As, over and over again,
You hear him climb
The ragged walk.

Every morning
My Head is pierced
With thorns

Because of yours
As, just beyond
The kitchen wall,

Persistent
Footsteps
Fall.

By your desire—
Still-born in the night—
My Side

Is lanced again,
Until blood and water
Come forth.

In this darkness,
You lie alone
With emptiness.

Your arms, like Mine,
Are cold . . .

Appalled to find themselves
Unable
To come together

To enfold your Love:
This is the Widow's cup
Of vinegar and gall.

Refuse it!
As I refused Mine.

It is useless—thoroughly—
To long
For what cannot be.

You have read this
Concerning Me:
It is finished!

* * * * *

It never is.

For Mrs. Marion Yurko

THE DONKEY AND THE WOMAN

O lowly Donkey! With what care you step
Between these stones not lightly tossed
By angry mountain gods to intercept

Travelers innocent of their domains;
With what fear you bray as into his trough
Swiftly sinks the sun, and day's light wanes.

Night now drops its terrors on this road,
Unfit for man or beast, yet you do not balk
At your encumbrance; nor at your awkward
load

Of pots and pans and swaddling clothes,
And the woman before her time—
That frail young girl first talked about
By Yahweh and by Isaiah—the *Virgin*

Whose promised Child even now moves
to be born,
So curious is He to see the world
His Father made on some yestermorn.

Alas! the Woman cries today, in '84,
God and World and Man—remade by man—
Find themselves effaceable. Who will be
our Guarantor?

The Child! *The Child*, now so anxious to see
night skies
Filled with stars that hang like flags unfurled
To guide; to sparkle; to shine, unmasked,
in lovers' eyes.

And one will shine, this night, o'er Bethlehem . . .

The time approaches, O Donkey! flat'ning
your ears,
Whereat the *Magnificant* labors to stem
Your tears, to comfort you, to touch your fears.

O Beastie!—so moved by her love—of all
on earth,
You will give your stall to the homeless Mother;
Your manger to bed her Son at birth.

You will see the Star; hear the angels' psalm;
Kick up your heels with joy at frankincense
and myrrh!
O favored Donkey! *You will walk, one day,*
on palm . . .

And, with the Woman, *wish the same for Man.*

EARLY CAME THE MAGDALENE

Before the great golden star strove
To forge into a nail-shaped clove
The despair of those dark nights

Since at the Cross she knelt aghast—
And now again at tomb, where last
In Black Friday's fading lights,

They laid Him in Joseph's linen
Nor din nor wind could enter in
So tight in place the great stone

Stood against the tomb. *The stone gone!*
The Lord gone! The dead, dead Lord. John!
Peter! Nor where is known.

Blackest waves, rising from below,
Dazed her mind. Strong the undertow
Of her lost, lost hope her grief.

Nor could she see the butterfly
Winging near and then close by
Settling green-gold on a leaf.

Unrecognized was the strange man
Who looked a garden's waterman—
A watering man in love.

Why dost weep so? Gently to her,
Thy tears this garden would water
As if they rained from above.

Mourning her Love, the Magdalene
Knew not His face, the Nazarene.
*Tell me where thou hast laid Him?**

The stricken sigh rose from the ground
A splinter from the ice that bound
Her heart in frozen hymn.

He called, then, her name in the tone
All love knows—knows its very own—
Mary! Only once. *Mary!*

Her cry traversed a flaming throat
Crossed by the sun's rising footnote
And stretched with love: *Rabboni!*

*St. *John, 20:15*

FEED MY LAMBS*

Undaunted long before 1965,
In deprived and pride-
Filled Mississippi, in
Biloxi—that song of songs
Singing beside the sea—

A mother, black and beautiful,
With unslacked fire blazing her soul,
Forged her boy into a man
Gentle, but strong, to survive
Without rancor
The harsh voyage of his life.

And as well, at her God-willed anvil,
She beat her own iron image
Into a drag anchor
To keep him headed into the wind.

Blessed be this mother
Who formed, in the Lord, a brother
With a heart so irresistible,
God called him to His altar.

On the day he embarked,
His Josephite brothers—
By whom he was taught
To keep his Star in sight

And his lines taut;
How to trim and mend his sails
To take advantage of the Wind—
Left on board his bark
A compass and its sea card
To guide him on his way.

Oh, the sweet irony of God!
Who *writes straight with crooked lines.***

That the same black hand,
Raised up to avoid disdain,
Should, this day, be the same
Black hand of the bishop
Raised up in blessing
Over Atlanta,
Asking God's favors to fall
In strict equality on all,
Both the benign and the unbenign.

That a child of a race
So long unseen and overseen
Should come by His grace
To this vast metropolis,
The King's overseer,
Carrying corn in his sack
For the hungered for justice;

To set a Table
With Bread and Wine
To feed His lambs,
And all those who have no home
Who will enter His House
To sit, side by side, together
In peace with one another.

To celebrate the
Installation of
The Most Reverend
Eugene A. Marino, S.S.J.
Third Archbishop of Atlanta;
First Black Archbishop
in the United States.
May 5, 1988

*The Archbishop's motto
**Portuguese proverb

*FROM INTIMATE IMPULSE**

Lying on a bed of thistle and thorn,
The archbishop wishes he'd never been born.
O promises unfulfilled! O bitter woe!
That so high a priest should fall so low.

Broken is the vow that set him apart
To rise—a star—in the southeast
Sky, to smile on black, alike on white.
And now—stripped of its glory hardly begun—
Is sucked into a deep and blackened hole.

Forfeit of his priestly vow, this man—once so fair—
Is Samson shorn of his miraculous hair.
Plucked out are the eyes that had blinked
At the flame of his shocking affair.
His spokesmen—embarrassed—spared themselves
        its name.
Yet visibly shamed were their euphemisms
Describing his orbital decay the while—
For days on end—he was the proscribed sport
Of the court jesters of the airwaves, of scribes.

O tragedy compounded! The woman
Was found to be no sweet Héloise,
Whose love for Abelard so pleased the poet.
The lady was a tramp—oh, bawdy song!—
A temple prostitute to the bishop belonged.

A contradiction was the lady of the
Sanctuary, who served Manna from Heaven
While afflicted with an addiction to cassocks.
Not one was found to be fireproof despite
The color of their piping. Molière
Gave a word for such characters—*tartuffe!*

Lo! How low fell this ruler in Israel . . .
The pillars of his integrity by
Himself pulled down and piled upon his head;
Destroyed, the charisma of his smile;
Scandalized, the sheep he promised to protect
From harm. *Feed My Lambs*—the motto ironic!
Yet newly emblazoned on his coat of arms.

Since the bishop's deception was exposed to men,
Waves of depression erode his heart. Darkness.
And—day and night—the eagle of his shame
Tears at the liver of his conscience.
Drawn from man's absurd pride, his feelings—
Non-healing—rise with such torment,
The abyss of a mind disjoined now yawns
For this priest anointed with holy oils for God.

Is there no deliverance for this man?
Is there no deliverance for the woman?—
Who might have become *another Magdalen*
Had the bishop remembered he'd been ordained
To be *another Christ* to remove the stain
Of sin. To make souls beautiful—like wool.

Yet his people loved him and, loving him,
Mourned this unexpected catastrophe—
Mourned for him like a death in the family.
He was their link to Rome; to the Apostles;
To their eternal destiny. Souls, souls. Oh, souls!

Now they would say to him: *Sorrow—nor remorse*
Nor shame—will release your tears for healing
Which God completes with His forgiveness—
Unasked—when His prodigals turn back Home.

*Milton's metaphor
for *concupiscence*

FULL OF AMAZEMENT

Faith stands
Full of amazement
At God's Love
Lying in a manger:
Miracle-Child, attuned to
Heaven and earth,
Born to seek,
Heal love; bind our wounds.

Swaddling
Bands restrain his feet
"Lest he bruise
Them against the harsh trough,"
Sweet Mary gravely explains.
(O, dear Mother—
Golden Ark—
You cannot save Him.)

He stretched
His arms wide in rose-
Blown circles
And caught a leaf off guard;
Clutched its beard, and touched its face,
As babies will.
And Mary
Smiled, as mothers will.

Sleep well,
Sweet mother. You, too,
Good Joseph.
God, his Father, will watch
His little Son. Doves roost, while
Angels—singing
Lullabies—
Close his sleepy eyes.

Tonight,
Like the shepherds, we
Come, filled with
Angels' song, dazed by light,
And stand *full of amazement:*
Lo! Asleep in
The feed-box
Lies God's pretty Lamb.

HERE AM I, LORD

Clap your hands! Clap your hands, O People
 of God!
Sing for your priest, Michael, now marking
 that day,
Two score years ago, when he was ordained with
 the power
To bless your joy, to console your sorrow; to free
Your soul of guilt, and to feed you at the altar.

For forty years, he has been graced to stand
 at the edge
Of wedded life, yet never to partake of it;
To smell the fragrance of the Rose, but never
 to pluck it.
To generate divine life in your babies at the font,
Yet never to have a child of his own.

Forty years! How swiftly they have passed! And
 even more
Since a child first climbed the altar of the Lord,
Stumbling over his cassock, scared half to death
While holding his breath over a cruet of water.

Lavabo inter innocentes . . .

Indeed, priests wash their hands among the
innocent,
And before none more innocent than this
acolyte:
A child chosen—before ever he was invited
To the womb—to become a priest of God;
to become
A son of Adam, flawed from the moment he
entered it,
Yet while still unborn, blessed in his flesh
with gifts:

An awesome love of God, to compel all to
His Christ;
An intellect, mercifully humble, to teach
His Law;
A smile, radiant and warm, to become
a fisher's net;
A voice, tender and sweet, to unpin men
and angels.
And oh, the memory! To greet, by name,
each member
Come to the Table to eat Supper with the family.

Not least of all was the gift of his ancestry,
With roots as wild as a snowdrift-in-the-making—
As unpredictable as a tempest at sea—
To be tamed, think Irish fathers and mothers,
By the priest down the street; by the Sanctuary.

There, one day, as if from a far-distant Shore,
The boy heard Someone calling his name.
        His name!
Like a wave from the Sea of Galilee,
The voice rolled over him:
MICHAEL! Come, follow me!
And the child replied:
Here am I, Lord.

For the 40th Anniversary of
Monsignor Michael J. Regan
May 30, 1986

*. . . I GIVE UNTO YOU**

Like icicles—succumbing to the sun—
Melt and drop from rooftop, trees,
The heart of man—shocked at being
Its Lord's golgotha—falls to its knees
At the sight of this Innocent.

Tender with the secrets of Heaven
Is the strengthening skull of the Infant,
Given—aye!—sired by God, and born the Son
Of Mary, without spot, without flaw,
On this holy and homeless night . . .

Wisdom! Beauty!—born of Beauty
On this homeless and holy night—
Inspiring men and women,
Children, and poets too;
Dividing history
And its time in two.

*John 14:27

ON THIS HOLY NIGHT

Maria! Cradle of Jesu Christi!
Echo of Yahweh's voice!
Radiance of the human race! Your soul's
Raiment through God's grace is
Your beauty, O Queen of Heaven!

Calyx of the Christ-Child! On this
Holy night, your petals unfold. *Behold*
 a white-winged
Rose revealing Love
Incarnate. Angels sing! Celestial cymbals ring!
Shepherds, trailing a star before, come
To adore Him. *Hail!*
Maid of Galilee! Dost hear again that
Angelic voice? *He shall be called the Son of God.*
Sweet Mother! I hear you whisper: "Sh,
 O Stars! My Baby sleeps."

JACOB'S LADDER
or
A Change in the Weather

The air was brisk—
As fresh as peppermint
In the mouth—
Nor rare, there

On that island—
Fish-shaped and
Long in the water—
East of New York, where

The deep blue scope
Of its autumn skies
Dazzles the eyes
At the end of September . . .
And clutches the throat
As if its beauty were
The one I remember.

Wonderfully content was I
Sitting on a catwalk and
Smelling the smell of boats . . .

Feeding the ducks
With crusts of bread—
The reward they expect
For walking on water.

I tasted salt
On my lips . . .
Cleansing. Deliquescent,
Like the heart-to-heart talk
Melting love,
Mending friendships.

I was in Paradise,
Which—alas!—
Does not last . . .
Nor ever
Since Adam was stigmatized.

For, the very next week,
As I stood in a house
On the water's edge,
Farther east,

I felt that cold blast
From the farthest North
That brought
A change in the weather.

The house still slept
As I stepped out
To test the chill,
Then wisely withdrew
Behind a window sill
To watch the sun rise
Over wetlands below.

Only to see,
Waiting on day,
The sky standing by

Holding a cup of cold tea—
Black and bitter—
With a couple of lemon peel
Floating in it.

But sleepy day
Would have none of it.
And before he knew it,
From his chin to his brow,
The face of the sky was trapped
In a black and angry cloud.

Yet there was hope
For a day nice and pretty
As the cloud—changing anew—
Dangled a piece of frayed rope
Or two.

Ah! Like the two fishes,
The two pieces multipled
One after another into rungs
Seen slowly stitched together.
Behold! A ladder leaned
Against the sky!

Oh, light that shone
Between those rungs!—
Nor green nor yellow,
But *blue!*—
The eyes of angels
Peering through.

Jacob's Ladder! . . .

That walkway from heaven
For angels—those thoughts
Of ours—who, even at this hour,
Ascend and descend—
Bearing the sense of God—
Our conscience—to the heart.

Intently, as had one of the three
Now tenting beneath a desert tree,
I followed the lights
Running up and down the sky.

Then, I *thought*
(O Angel! What sense is this?)
I heard the voice of One
Sitting on the uppermost rung
Or was it a bell tolling?—
I could not tell
For, the tone I heard
Belonged to Jacob's son,

Meant to be left for dead
In the pit of an ancient well,
But—strange pity of his brothers!
Sold—a slave—instead.

Eerie was the sound
Of that voice—
Haunting—
Like the one I found
Rocking in the sea
Around a golden isle . . .

Like the unutterable note
Hovering over friendship—
Once closer than air—
Left uncovered, vulnerable—
Stripped bare
Of its multicolored coat.

* * * * *

Suddenly! The ladder collapsed.
And the sky was filled with glory
As in the old, old story.

I stood enrapt,
Hearing a Bell rung
In a hillside cave . . .
Echoing back forever
From another Hill—

I forgave. I forgave.
Can you not do as well?

* * * * *

Darkness fell—
As black as space is black.

From the edge of the Wind,
I heard the voice of the Lord
Who made the wind. It was
As sharp as hunger
Under a double-edged sword

For me, for us,
For all the world
Changing forever—
Like the weather—
From darkness to light, and
Back to darkness again,

I trembled
Like the morning
For, stinging Man's face
Like none other
Was the Lord God's warning . . .

You shall not see My Face
Except you bring your brother
*With you.**

*Genesis 43:5

A POPE FROM POLAND

Your Poland knows—
As did Peter, that other firebrand—
We must obey God,
Nor be afraid of man.

Your Poland's faith, that wept at a crematorium,
Is now the jeweled sword of His Church,
Brandishing before Istanbul,
Demanding freedom for all.

With awakened hope, we look
To you—our Pope,
Selected by the Spirit—
To dispel the clouds that darken the world;

To search out our brothers who cry for food;
To bring the Living Water to those others,
Half-dead from thirst.
Who starve for the Bread of Heaven.

To commemorate
the Investiture of
Pope John Paul II,
the first non-Italian pope in 455 years,
October 22, 1978

JESUS! EMMANUEL!

His birth-cry, that startled a star-dented sky,
Is quiet now. Jesus—as yet unharmed—
Lies fast asleep in His Mother's arms.
O Embodiment of the Highest Good!

You are the hope of Man for God's forgiveness,
The hope of Woman for Mary's fearlessness.

Yet now, as if this Child were never born,
Man glorifies his self-seduction
And vaunts his pride
In his self-destruction.

O Man! O Woman! Is it not time
To look into the looking-glass?

Dare we be less humble than our God
Who forsakes His Heaven to repair our loss?
Is birthed among cattle when He comes to earth—
Helpless—dependent on a woman's breast?

Who dies—in the end—upon a shameful cross
For our sake? For our sake?

In all of history, only Jesus
Did this for us!
No one—no one by any other name—
Did this for us!

Read! Oh, read! Can we find a single name?

What man? What woman? (You? I?)
Would willingly die for all the souls on earth
Regardless of race, of color, wealth, or sex?
Of intellect, of place or time of birth?

Only a god would do this!
Only a god could do this!

Hear, all ye peoples! There is but one God.
Hear, O Israel! The Lord, thy God, is One.
Emmanuel! *God with us!* Jesus!
Who needed Man's tears

To weep over Jerusalem,
To weep over us.

JOSEPH

Green and wild are cedared hills
When, on her wedding eve,
The Virgin avows God's only Child.

O startling discovery,
Grieving faithful Joseph!
How? How? How can this ever be?

Is it fantasy that hides
Her shame? Ill-begotten
Is his thought. She could be maimed—killed!—

If in public, he disowns
The maid: So wroth and quick,
The stones in wronged Semitic hands.

I will put her away, quietly.

Then it is he hears the Virgin cry:
Adonai! O Adonai!
How hard it is to bear Thy Child!

But not yet does Joseph understand;
Not now, nor later in his house,
So incredulous is his heart.

But God, Who holds most dear the just,
Sends an angel to Joseph's dream
To glean the reaping of his tears,

To say to him: *Fear not, Joseph,*
To take Mary for thy wife:
The Life begun is God's own Son.

* * * * *

Thus, and when, in David's Bethlehem,
A carpenter signs an infant's name:
Jesus of Nazareth, Son of Mary

And, he whispers to the Wind,
Of God.

JOSEPH, FOLLOW ME!

The Lord, when first He saw you, called,
Joseph, follow Me!
And you responded, leaving all
To serve—away and far from home—
Christ's neglected poor.
And found Him crucified again.

Today, become His consecrated Knight,
You bear His standard now for life. So armed
With mighty lance, your sacred charge,
You ride to lists—empowered stole aloft—
To joust with Satan, Angel once of Light,
Through pride (O Sin!) in darkness plunged
To hell, apart
From God forever more.

Then Man was made to take his place,
Given light to shine
As once it did to the banished Prince
Who—fiercely lonely—strives to snare
Souls to share, in grief,
His dreadful hole. (He'd found in Man
The loophole—God's gift of choice in will.)

Not satisfied with Paradise destroyed,
He still entices men to taste
Of fruit forbidden; plans by stealth to rob
Their prize, garroting souls with honeyed talk—
His hangman's noose—though loosed by Christ,
A dangling strand
Still threatening Damocles.

The Son of God alone
Did cause the Fiend to tremble, flee
His victim, run amuck.

Once more—today—he's struck
As visors lift, and lo! he sees,
In yours, the Face of Christ.

Alleluia!

To celebrate the ordination
of Father Joseph J. Donovan, M.M.
At Maryknoll, New York
May 19, 1979

THE KING OF ISRAEL

What did Israel expect to see? . . .
A king wearing a golden crown
Upon his head? Or helmeted
And carrying a sword?

The king, the deliverer, is at hand!

Words transposed—or lost like waifs
As they crossed the Jordan—
Created the rumor for a Jerusalem
Chafing under the yoke of Rome.

O blessed hope! O blessing joy!

Men—all Israel—wept,
Like a woman too long sleeping alone
Weeps to see her longed-for lover
Standing at her door.

The news swept through the underground,
Setting new fires under the Zealots—
Those patriots already burning
To be free. Already fire-hot.

With an armful of rocks, they stalked
The enemy to out-of-the-way places.
Smashed his smooth imperial face.
Crushed his Roman skull.

Under the walls, they pounced on sentries,
        oft alone
And fearful of beards stiff with eaglets' blood.
Garotted to his last breath,
The soft thud pronounced him dead.

Unlike David's lethal pebble,
The Zealots' attacks—so brave and rash—
Were but the nibblings of mice:
Goliath would prevail.

But at last—totally aghast at their droppings—
Rome flushed the bold rebels out of their holes . . .
Their agony, alas! the portent
Of the saddest event in history . . .

Barabbas already jailed
Even as a carpenter
Walked out of the water.

TO THE MOTHER OF HEAVEN
FOR THE CHILDREN OF EARTH

Virgin! whose shining star tames the wild sea's
Ire, draw into your fire the hate
Raging through the world. Men's fever abate.
Gather within your white light the disease
Infecting mankind, the harsh jealousies
Nagging this agony. Illuminate,
Immaculate Mother! O, roseate
Amethyst! Sober man's inanities.

Mary!

Mother! You can change those who
know you not:
Each and everyone in Arabia;
Each fighting Christian deaf to children's cries,
Having His voice and your echo forgot.
Ah! May your flame define their golgotha:
Nahum dooms whilst, once more,
your Christ-Child dies.

Christmas, 1977

LET THY LIGHT RISE UP IN THE DARKNESS*

An Easter Cantata

We turn our backs,
We turn our backs on the Lord
For evil acts and passions without love.

Unsteady we stand
Muddied with obscenity,
Mired in pornography.

Blessed is the one who loves the Lord!

We despise our own flesh:
And the naked unborn expire
Without crèche or warm garment.

We care not for the harborless
Nor bring them into our house
To share our anxious bread.

Blessed is the one who loves the Lord!

Nor will with proper words fill
The minds of daffodil children,
So blind are we to their blossoming.

Do as we say, not as we do—
And our own ears, sundered by the Bard's brew,
Hear not the thunder in the hearts of our children.

Blessed is the one who loves the Lord!

We dare to demand forgiveness
When there is none, nor gentleness,
In our own hearts, in our own hearts.

We flake married love, even friendship,
Harrying our mates without mercy
For failings we know are under our own gloves.

Blessed is the one who loves the Lord!

Divorce! Devastating divorce without thought
Of the course unfolding for a child
Stunned by the drought of our love.

Such fragile souls are they
Who bear the ill wind
Buffeting their shoaled parents.

Blessed is the one who loves the Lord!

We defile ourselves
In the sight of God.
We trod upon that which is not our own:

Our neighbor's wife.
His goods. His very life
Belabored with gun and knife!

Nor is that enough!
Even after he is dead,
We rough up his bed with laughter.

Blessed is the one who loves the Lord!

Gold is our god.
We fleece it from all, even the old.
Even the poor. We cheat even the poor.

Nor do we satisfy the afflicted,
The sick, the aged, the addicted,
Whose tears stalk their eyes, their very breath.

Unconcerned, unmoved, everyone
Turns aside to his own way.
Like sheep, we go astray.

Blessed is the one who loves the Lord!

By the works of our own hands
We provoke Him;
Nor know this is the stroke of death.

We lie to ourselves that we have no sin. We lie.
Fearful of His discipline,
We adhere not to the Lord.

Blessed is the one who loves the Lord!

Who calls to us:

> *Seek Me, all of you, with your heart*
> *Do not depart from Me.*
>
> *Stretch forth your hand,*
> *You shall not forget, nor shall I,*
> *If you but put it into My side.*
>
> *Be not faithless.*
> *Aye! Be not faithless,*
> *But believing. It is I*
>
> *Who was crucified*
> *And am risen.*
> *Here I am. Here I am, open-eyed . . .*
>
> *To forgive you,*
> *To give you a new heart*
> *And a new spirit within you.*
>
> *I was bruised and broken for you.*
> *Choose not to turn your eyes from Me.*
> *Who else will burn your sins and open up your grave?*

The stone has been rolled out and away
from your soul.
Shout! Shout! Shout with joy! Shout with joy!
You are free. You are free. You are free.

Give Me your right hand. Nor leave your
left one idle.
In bridal array, hold on to your sister,
your brother.
Through you, I say, My love will find another.

Take My hand. We shall talk. We shall be
silent.
We shall sing together on my planet,
in my lovely world.
I am sent to walk hand in hand with you.
This is My joy!

Your face will shine
As a light to others;
And your speech will be as sweet wine

To refresh your sisters,
To relax your brothers.
You will enmesh their souls for Me

With charity and love.
For where there is charity and love,
God is there. God is there. God is there.

Before the beginning of time, I was
your Friend.
Now, from this moment, you are Mine.
Now and forever, world without end. Amen.

For this is the day which the Lord has made.
And the land shall rejoice and bring forth
its fruits in gladness.
And its days shall not be destroyed.
Days shall be added to it.

Alleluia! Alleluia! Alleluia!

*Based on Isaias 58:10, (Douay Version)

THE LONELY ALBATROSS

Let hope lift up our hearts!
The tremendous darkness
Of our abyssal world
Is pierced through,
This night,
By dazzling arcs of light
Sent forth by angels appointed

To spread a sprig of mistletoe
Above our dispirited heads:
To bring the kiss of God to us
In remembrance now
Of His most gracious gift of all
When the Lord endowed the human race,
So parched for love before,
With His beloved Son.

We adore Thee, O Christ!

And bless the Virgin
Who fleshed the Word.
And praise her,
The vessel of Israel's expectation,
Who sheltered our Consolation.

Blest be the holy night
Filled with blinding light.
Blest, the earth
Adorned with glory
The night that Christ was born.

Hark! The counterpoint
Beneath the angels' song:
The sound of a Tree
Breathing in the wind,
Shaking with sighs
Over the mystery
Of this comely Child,
The King of Kings,

Who will become—
Ever after
His long, narrow wings
Are pinioned to the spar-arms
Of a Cross—

The lonely Albatross
Haunting the sails of Life
And its vaunting sailors,

Forever.

THE LORD IS RISEN, AS THE WOMEN SAID

The grave is empty?
He is risen, you say?

Their eminence offended,
The Eleven and the others
Would not believe
The women's tale.

Nonsense! they cried,
Disdainful that women
Could be divinely ordained
To carry tidings from the Lord.

And blocked were their eyes
When, that very night,
Jesus came through doors
Shut tight and locked.

O ye! So slow of faith!
No wraith am I.
Touch my flesh!
Feel my bones!

Yet did they hesitate . . .
Then said their Guest:

That you may know
I truly live,

Give me something to eat.
And they gave Him a boneless fish,
Broiled and sweetened with honey.
And He ate.

Only then did their eyes
Shed their scales. He is risen!
Alleluia! Alleluia!
The Lord is risen, as the women said.

Based on Luke, Ch. 24
NAC Edition

MY BELOVED SON

Truly was Our Lady fair.
With chips of cedar in her soul,
She was—the poet wrote—
*Our tainted nature's solitary boast.**

Prepared by the King of the Universe
For the sake of His heavenly heir,
She was preserved from sin—as pure
As—in the beginning—Eve had been.

Strange. He spared her not from pain.
Behold! At that dramatic moment
She shared with mothers everywhere,
A tear dropped into the manger, where

In the folds of human skin
God's divinity lay hidden
Like beauty in the heart
Of a rose unopened . . .

His infinity bound
By the bounds of man
Like mystery enclosed
In a folded fan.

*Idle tales*** (ask Magdalene),
Would say the men of Israel . . .

Gabriel? Hah! A wild imagining!
God fathering her child? Bah!

And Mary—mother while yet a child—
Wisely locked her secret in her heart.
According to His will, it had been done.
God Himself must acknowledge His son.

Silent would the virgin be.

Patiently for thirty years she waited,
While Jesus—smoting nails each day except
The seventh—was spoken of as the carpenter . . .
Hailed as the son of Joseph.

Yet the virgin remained silent.

Suddenly, Jesus was gone! Left home
To wander throughout Israel—
Homeless and without a shekel among strangers.
Mary wept, sensing danger.

Something had been said
About some news for the Jews . . .
About forgiveness. What if He said
*I and the Father are one?****

Now disraught, the mother was wroth
With the Father . . . His son—*her* son!—
Sent on a most perilous mission
Without the proper credential!

With both hands she grasped an idle hammer
And broke the silence of all those years unspoken.
Nor asked, but demanded His answer.
This very day—how would she know?—

Jesus was standing in the river Jordan.

There—even this moment—the heavens opened
And the children of Abraham heard
The voice of the distant *I* AM.
Not on a flame from a burning bush,

But on a rush of wings, it came
To hover over the head of Jesus,
To cover him with glory—seen by those
Whose fathers had seen a divided sea.

From far beyond the Pleiades,
The Faceless Voice addressed
The virgin's son—blessing
Forever the mother waiting . . .

Thou art my beloved Son,
*In whom I am well pleased.*****

*William Wordsworth
**Luke 24:11 (King James)
***John 10:30 (ibid.)
****Mark 1:11 (ibid.)

*MY STONES CRY OUT TO YOU**

My stones cry out to you:
Come, dear children, beloved of Christ,
And hear how, through
The words of His Church, you will be enticed

To the discovery
Of your Faith; for without hearing
You can have no guarantee of heaven;
And the devil will be leering.

My stones cry out to you,
Our Lady's children:
Come! Learn the derring-do
Of God's love for you when

He sent the Christ, His Son,
To suffer, to die for you and me, for *all* of us.
From perpetual darkness He won
Our souls through that bloody sacrifice,
so piteous.

The great mystery of God
Is love for all that He has made:
Love for you, your parents, your cat, your dog,
and golden-rod;
Your brothers and sisters and your old maid
aunt;

For your playmates; even for the schoolyard
Bully. And for your priests, your teachers,
And the school-crossing guard.
With love, too, for the pom-pom girls,
        and their parents in the bleachers.

My stones cry out to you:
Find this wondrous God in what you hear here.
And go forth and find Him too
In the joy of others and in the fear

And want of those who suffer,
For God says: *Look for Me there.*
And in the sinner and in the bluffer,
In the ugly and in the fair.

For the Lord says: *I am there.*

My stones cry out to you:
Let the light of God, that will be flamed by me,
Shine through you.
Let it become—oh! let it *be*

The beacon by which you will set
Your course in life: Let it be a harbor-light
To others who may be beset
By the waves of temptation. And let it free them
        from their fright.

To you, my children, my stones cry out:
Come! Learn to live in peace and forgiveness.
Know! Do not doubt
That I shall teach you patience and kindness.

Learn from me that your sin,
Your rebellion against God, will harm you
Not only, but all your kin,
Your friends, and the very Church that nurtures
    you!

Here in my shelter, you and your parents also
Can enjoy your songs and dances,
Your games and contests. Your shows
And all your wonderful extravaganzas.

For here too in fun as well as in prayer,
He is with you, and nothing pleases Him more
Than that His children, big and little, bestir
    the air
With their liveliness and adore

Him with their joy. For you are
His brothers and His sisters, His very own family;
And He would play with you as He does
    with the morning star
And would have you roam the skies—but
    not forget the Tree.

So, in knowledge and joy, I will provide
You with the map and the food,
With the light and the fire to sustain and guide
You on your life's journey, His planned prelude

To the unimagined happiness in His Home
Where the littlest angel rolls his hoop
And delights the Virgin with his jewelled comb.

Stone and wood and the sweat
Of your parents created me
For you, Our Lady's children, to set
The tone of your lives, to teach you how to *be*.

Dedication of
CHARLES CARROLL CENTER
by the Most Rev. Thomas A. Donnellan,
November 6, 1977

*Inspired by Luke 19:40

A SONG TO GOD

O Praise the Lord, the Lord our God,
Creator of earth and heaven.
He made all things. And like unto Him,
God made us Man and Woman.
With lights and stars He filled the skies,
The falling night, the morning's rise.
All wants and needs He satisfies.
We sing a song to God.

O Thank the Lord, the only Son of God.
For us He was scourged and crucified.
O Christ, our Lord, to You the rod,
The Kingdom's gates to ope wide.
Your death gave us the victory.
We worship You, Who set us free.
O let us share the Sacred Tree.
We sing a song to God.

O Praise to the Lord, the Holy Light,
The flame of the Blessed Trinity.
O wonderful Love so pure, so bright,
Who found the Virgin worthy.
O Lover, come to us as promised us.
To You, the Son entrusted us.
All children of God victorious,
We sing a song to God.

Chorus:
Loved, beloved are we,
Whose lives are in Your Hand, Lord.
Great Hope of Paradise,
Who set us free,
All glory to You, Lord Christ.
Your blessings on us do You impart;
Keep friends and family within Your Heart,
O Son of God, O Star of Morn,
As with Our Lady, Maria,
We sing a song to God.

STAND STILL! TURN AROUND AND LOOK AT ME!

Ah! My friend, bowed down
Under the hod of your sin,
Why do you walk *into* the wind?

For your sake, I
—The Son of God—
Left My abode with Him
To become the Son of Man:
To become your Serving-Man
And relieve you of that heavy load.

Here's where your burden lies:
In the Cross upon My back.
Here's where your sin lies:
In the Blood that runs like sweat
Into My eyes.

Though I follow you,
I cannot catch up with you.
You latch on to your own will
And walk into the wind.

Put the wind at your back!

Stand still! Turn around.
And *look* at Me!

Seat of Wisdom

Bronze, 20″ H.

Henry Setter, Sculptor

THRONE OF CHRIST
(Seat of Wisdom)

Alone unmarked by Eden's scar,
The designated Virgin sits
Unmovable in her motherhood.
Impregnated are her eyes—filled!

With the royal message she has heard
That rapturized her will to God's.
O unproved, unprovable Prelude
That brought forth from Heaven's court

The Everlasting Word,

Who now, in human flesh,
Inhales the first sweet scent
For Everyman: the fragrance
Of His mother's breast.

O Adam, yet ensnared by self-deceit,
Cast out your shame! Rise! Soar!
Enthroned upon so rare a seat,
Grace—unasked—is there:

The Christ-Child,

True God from true God,
Enlivened by the Spirit;
One in essence with the Father,
But with His Mother's eyes,

Who now exhales
God's breath divine,
And yours . . . and yours . . .
And mine.

Inspired by the sculpture
Seat of Wisdom
by Henry Setter

THE UNCONVERTED

Christ stands
Beside our unrolled stone,
And weeps for those
He hopes to call His own.

Come forth!
He cries to those of us
Whose dead souls
He'd return to life.

But some of us,
Whose eyes have grown accustomed
To the total gloom
Of our customed, self-made

Tomb,
Know we cannot stand
The Light,
And so refuse.

WHEN DEATH IS ECSTASY*

Dyland Thomas would not have us
Go gentle into that good night;
Nor would Edna St. Vincent Millay,
Whose candle, burning at both ends,
Lit up my Village days
And flamed their nights.
She was not resigned. Nor, then, was I.

But Death is not what it seems;
It is not as they said.
It's the little foxes, instead,
Who abort our dreams.
It's the little foxes, the plague
And blight of mortal life,
Who sneak beneath the gate
To spoil the vines
And harden the tender grape.

Even now, dear Friend, so ill,
They would obtain one last foray:
In shadows, red and bold,
They wither your bed.
They trample your body until
Your toes curl up in pain . . .

A pain, nevertheless, far less
Than the ache in your heart
That led you on that endless search—
Climbing up the Palm Tree,
To see Him through Its boughs;
Trudging the weary miles
Through cities of children—
Looking for the God of your vows
Who, you sometimes thought,
Had abandoned you.
(So, appalled, you thought.
So did Jesus. So do we all.)

Oh, how you remembered
The apple-smell of Him!
It was in your nose
And on your clothes.

And everywhere you went,
You trailed the lovely scent
Of lilies-of-the-valley,
Whose chaliced perfume
Rose up from their green bed
Where first He looked at you
And found you fair;
Where He called you
My Beloved . . .
And your arms encircled
His Head.

And now, sweetening
These tense moments,
And stronger than ever before,
Is the smell of His ointments
In the air. O Friend so fair!
Let all else be still . . .
See! Your Lover comes to you,
Leaping upon the mountains,
Skipping over the hills.

And when He kisses you
With the kiss of His mouth,
You will be in Heaven.

*Inspired by the courage of
Sister Mary Teresa Penner, O.P.
as seen in the *Song of Solomon.*

AN UNEXPECTED TRIP TO BETHLEHEM

No matter lovely Mary's time had come,
Caesar must be obeyed. Did not the Child,
Become a man, spell out the maximum
Due Caesar? The decree was nationwide.

This was a boy who bulged out her body.
From her high carriage, woman knows the child
Who will become a man. But this plod-y
Journey o'er roads mountainous, rough, and wild?

It would take more than a week, with Joseph
Walking every step of the way. O, *Lord!*
Incline Thine ear toward me. Do not be deaf
To my plea for our Son. In accord

With Thy Word, He was conceived and cared for.
Let no harm come to Him now after all
This time Lord! Thine angel send forth before
Us to guard Joseph and the Babe so small.

* * * * *

Fear not, sweet Mary, My hand will support
Your aching back and although you dismount
your donkey,
Mount and mount again, transport
You safely he will for he knows the fount

Of his blessed Burden and already
Worships Him, the Christ, his little Brother.
Steady he will be enroute, and sturdy be
For the sake of the Child and His Mother.

Nor need you fear that a field strange and rough
On the side of a road lonely and wild,
Nor its scraggly weeds will become the stuff
Of bed for the birth of this wondrous Child.

I do promise you here no more, yet more,
Than shelter for you from the wind's cold bite
When to Bethlehem you come: Golden Tau,
My brightest star, will be your acolyte

To light up the night sky for miles around
To guide shepherds, kings, to the beasties' cave
Where, with you and Joseph, He will be found—
The Flawless Wheat that man henceforth will crave.

WE KNOW YOU BY YOUR NAME

What do we call You, Lord?
How express, except in clumsy metaphor,
The mystery of the Primal Force?

A seamless, featureless
Beginning with no beginning!

Out of nothing, You brought forth
The boundless universe. Lamped it.
Dispersed galaxies into endless space.
Made man a face . . .
And eyes
Out of the dust of stars.

What do we call You, God?

With no material form,
You are, like air,
Invisible and everywhere.
And not the same, in any way,
As a man.

Yet—oh, heavenly paradox!—
You *are* seen, O Lord,
In Man's unseen,
Immortal soul.

Moses claimed
A flame on Horeb
Revealed Your name.
To this son of Abraham,
He said You said

I AM WHO AM

And that,
When You commanded him
To Egypt to free the Jews,
You ordered him to stand
At a distance from You . . .
And to take off his shoes.

Maybe it was the way he said it?
You became a god of plagues,
And of punishment; a god of war,
Leading Israel to victory . . .
A split personality, really,
For another said
You were a god of mercy,
And still another
That You were like a mother.

Then—oh, heavenly intervention!—
When You sent Your Word
To be fleshed of the Virgin,

To free Man
From a greater affliction,

It was *You*
Who stood at the portal
Of that singular maid.
It was *You*
Who waited
On her word.

Ah, immaculate consent!

At which Your Word—
The same Word through Whom
All light and life began—
The Son of God—of God, the same—
Became the Son of Man

Come to tell Man, You are
The Godhead—the Trinity—
One God, and Lord of Love
Forevermore.

Yet Jesus,
As true man,
Was limited by His times;
Was frustrated by the anguish
Of human language.

What would He call You?

You are incorporeal
And not, in any way,
As a man . . .
Would He find
The one name for You
Babel could understand?

Ah, how appropriate
Was His metaphor for You,
O Generator of Life!

The Lord Jesus,
As man,
Called You

Father . . .

WOMAN AND THE FIRST CHRISTMAS*

O Woman! Forbidden by men of old,
Even to today—even to her, who
Was half of earth and half of heaven—
To enter the Holy of Holies,

Unfreeze your treasures.
Leap up! O Windrows of the Holy Spirit,
Lying idle in white fields in heaps of gold
And silver; of diamonds, emeralds, and rubies.

Bounty of the blowing Wind,
Your gifts will yet enrich Christ's Church,
How odd that men would stay you still,
would say
God does not will that you offer them at
the altar.

Your pain is splintered
From the pauper-Christ's (so God disclosed
His Son in Adam's clothes): He, too,
was subject
To scorn, rejected by (quote, unquote)
authority.

Take courage in the fact
That when He, *Whom the heavens could not*
contain,
Came to earth, the Lord chose the corridor
Of a woman for His birth. And in her *Fiat*

That enabled the
Incarnation of God, the Son;
That gave voice and heart to Him; a choice
to women
And to men; to every nation, hope for salvation.

What's more—*glory to women!*—
The Lord, in order to vest Himself in
Human flesh, chose to enter the abode that He—
Not man—had made: The Holiest of Holies,

A woman's womb,

The sacred scabbard
Of the Divine Sword of Heaven that,
Unsheathing, left intact the Mother's virgin-life,
As is every virgin's under a surgeon's knife.

O Double Miracle of that Birth—nay, Triple!—
That brought God's Joy out of Mary's womb,
Where our sister—not by God disdained—
Also *by Himself was ordained*

To celebrate, by Heaven's Authority,
The first Christ's Mass, Christmas!
When she changed the pre-existent Logos,
Without His losing His Divine Identity,

Into the Body and the Blood of Jesus.

*Christmas from Old English
Cristesmaesse (Mass of Christ)

THE DIVINE BARGAIN

In exchange for your childlike heart,
I will give you the morning star.
Woulds't come, John Paul?
It was past nightfall, Luciani smiled.

* * * * *

When men found him at dawn,
They were stunned by the
Ray of the sun playing
Like a finger of Venus on his lips.

In memory of
Pope John Paul I:

The meteor that lit up
the heavens for 33 days,
then disappeared on
September 28, 1978

PETER TO PAUL VI*

Rome was my last home too,
And became my tomb as it does for you
Today.

I, too, died outside its walls—
Scoffed by men engulfed in their
Own lusts.

Even then, among our own, were some—
Though washed in the waters of Christ—
Whose ears

Twitched to false prophets
And lying teachers. Who
Worshipped

Gold before God. Who learned,
Alas! only on the doorstep
Of death,

The emptiness of high-sounding words
Cloaked in freedom's banner to
Entice them

By sensual images to debauchery.
Whose greed deprived the poor. Then,
As now,

They were like dogs returning to
        their own vomit;
Like pigs after wallowing in the
Mire.

Who surrendered their bodies
To adultery, drunkenness, drugs; and
Defiled

Their God-given lives, once redeemed,
In revelings, carousings, in
Orgies.

Your world, Paul, has returned to the
Darkness of mine. I was a lamp
Shining

In that dark place as you were in yours,
A beacon to the sheep to return to the
Shepherd.

I, too, was spoken of
In disparagement when I fought for
My Master.

The commandment I myself received
From the Lord I passed through time
To you.

For the love of Christ, I died.
And you—you were crucified in
Your heart.

You were not alone, dear Paul.

Before you,
I, *Peter*,
was there.

In memory of
His Holiness, Pope Paul VI

On the day of his entombment
St. Peter's, Rome
August 12, 1978

*Based on the Epistles of St. Peter

†THOMAS

and His Knights

Step softly at this holy spot,
O mournful procession . . .
Hold back that tear
As you pass this bier
Whereon your bishop lies.

See the crow's feet
That quote his Irish eyes?
He would not have you weep,

But pray for him. For, even now,
Behind that unlocked door,
The Owner of the flock
Asks His shepherd: *How deep*
Was your love for My sheep?
How well did you feed them?
And My lambs? Protect them?
And rescue the stray
From the marauding Wolf?

For Thomas, face-to-face with God,
This is his moment of truth . . .

While on the other side of the door,
The honored Knights
Stand guard,
With their white-plumed helmets
And shining swords reflecting
The four-horned candlelight.

They stand—proud and stiff
As Swiss Guards—yet not unmindful
Of the Judgment: for them, too,
Their bishop is accountable.

Oh, memory—that will never end—
Of Light that humbles hearts
And glazes over eyes!

As from a roof in Damascus,
The Knights descend
Their final watch,

Nor ever before so close
To Christ, the Lord. To Jesus!

O sudden Insight—
Grace amazing to receive!—
To gaze upon their bishop's hands
And perceive the shepherd's power
Given Thomas in his golden hour:
The divine right from the Nazarite
To feed His lambs, to feed His sheep—

A laser light
Piercing centuries,

Handed down—unbent—
Hand over hand to bishops—
To Thomas—from, and as granted,
Those twelve most intimate friends.

In memory of
Most Rev. Thomas A. Donnellan
1914 - 1987
Archbishop of Atlanta
1968 - 1987

HIS PRESENCE

Where [one], two of you, or more
Glorify My Father
In His House, or in yours,
There I am in your midst.
So I told you. Ah!
My sister! My brother!
I Myself exalt your prayers—
Gold-spun
Now, for our Father.

At home, at work, at play—
Everywhere!—I am there
Beside you. I share your pew
At God's service.
I sit close to you,
Next to you. And at the
Kiss of Peace, see Me! Give Me
Your hand.
Trust Me: I am there.

Then

At the door of My tent,
I'll bathe your dusty feet.
From the North, South, West, or East,
Whencesoever you come,

I shall embrace you.
And your mouth will be sweet
As honey when I kiss you,
My love,
At My Feast. Shalom!

For Mary Benchina
July 3, 1980

BALANCING ACCOUNTS

No need to be wordy with God
All the livelong day.
Appeal to Him a package deal
At the start of every day.

Offer all the assets
To be accumulated—
Joys anticipated—
And liabilities yet to be encumbered—
The sorrows least and most expected—
Banshees that continually wail
Outside the counting house.

Turn over to Him
The debts incurred, and owed
With promissory notes
Given for borrowed love.
And be assured, God insures
That He will honor them.

Nor will He fail
To liquidate the sin
Which, repented and forgiven,
Brings souls closer to Him.

Wrap this all up
And tie it with work
In field, at desk,
Or in the kitchen—
Wherever it may rest.

For all accounts,
Both large and small,
Are safely in His charge
And faithfully balanced
At the end of every day.

Nor would He write off
To Doomsday
The penny lost or strayed,
But works overtime
To find it, each and every time.

Next morning, with shining Face,
God gives a fresh start
With a profit brought forward
From the bottom line
Of yesterday's report . . .

And traced
To *grace.*

IS MAN TO DOMINATE HEAVEN TOO?

Or Provisos for a
Spiritual Equal Rights Amendment,
S.E.R.A., for Catholic Women

Heaven, you've been told, is conquered
 by violence.
And so it seems. Before I was four,
My head was filled with the consequence
Of becoming a saint: He was thrown to the
 lion's jaw—

Or crucified upside down.
Stoned. Stretched on a wheel like my own
 Catherine.
Steeped in boiling oil until his skin
 flaked brown.
Beheaded. Stabbed under the very altar's
 baldachin.

The most painful image of all
For anyone, and especially a young girl,
Was that of the God-Son—to Whom surely
 nothing evil could befall—
Dead on a cross of pearl. Dead on a cross
 of pearl.

Before reading was officially on my agenda,
On visits to Grandfather I was enthralled
by a book
I found on his reading table. Its name:
Heiligen Legende—
The story of the saints—and worthy of a very
private nook,

Where I was fascinated by its pictures—
each saint had his own
And each had his own day of the year.
To a curious Catholic child, violence comes
early and full blown;
I was too young to know love, but not
too young to know fear.

It takes years to understand
That the killing of saints comes not from God
But that it comes from the man
Who would be a demi-god.

After Grandfather died and the book
Became mine, I could read:

Ich bin der Herr euer Gott, seid helig
Weil Ich heilig bin!
"I am the lord Thy God, be holy
As I am holy!"

In such lofty tones, He calls to you
in every language.
Nor can any of you become holy obliquely.
Your heart and soul must build, *straight up*,
the bridge
On which you will know His Presence uniquely.

Such awareness in a priest
Makes him truly what he is called:
the *alter Christus,*
Who continues the work from south to north,
from west to east,
To which Christ gave the glorious stimulus.

Such awareness in you, whether or not
a mother,
Makes you truly what you are entitled
to be called: The *altera Maria.*
For where Christ is, there also is Mary,
His Mother,
And your work will be like hers: a living,
resounding Gloria!

Besides, in doing ordinary things
extraordinarily well,
You may yet merit canonization.
John Neumann did exactly this.
Madame and Mademoiselle!
The time has come for equalization

With men in the Calendar of the Saints!
Of the three hundred sixty-five pictures I
looked at as a child,
Only seventy-five (seventy-five!) were those
of female saints
And to this you should never be reconciled.

You shall not abandon
Sweeping the sanctuary,
Laundering cassocks and altar linen,
Polishing marble, candlesticks, and statuary;

Preparing covered dishes, baking cake,
And sorting used clothing.
Nor shall you forsake
The nursery and Sunday School teaching.

For these things can, in His name, merit you
Eternal Life;
But they will not win you official recognition
From Rome. Just being a good housewife
Bent on some charitable mission,

In the eyes of the Church, is not enough,
Although you know—and I know it—
With a husband and children,
sometimes the going can be rough
And quite heroic.

Today, with your awakened intelligence,
Will you permit men only to be recognized,
In this world and the next, for pre-eminence
Of Soul? Souls are created equal. They are
equally exercised

By the Holy Spirit. Be conscious of the Lord
While you go about your ordinary tasks;
And as you work in a hospital or a prison ward.
Be aware of His Presence as you help unmask

The evil and injustices in the world.
Fight for human rights; for birthright!
Fight the underworld,
Its insidious pornography and drugs. Light,

Light more than a candle—*light the sky!*—
With your efforts for world peace
and tranquility.
Yourself and others sanctify. Youth purify.
Help the poor overcome their vulnerability.

Release the aged from their fear
Of poverty; from their overpowering loneliness.
Encourage the girl in trouble, the reluctant
woman
To persevere, to avoid abortion's vicious
emptiness.

Watch sharply legislators; and proposed
legislation:
See to it that it is beneficial to your society,
Not to selfish interests; nor that it is an
abrogation
Of our God-given liberty.

The foreign student needs your assistance;
so does the refugee.

Through these last two alone,
All differences notwithstanding,
With hope for your survival and that
of your hearthstone,
You can improve international understanding.

With His help, all this—heaven too—
can be attained
If you remember Whose Hand you hold;
And you may yet be inscribed in the roster
of the saints
If, for His sake, you are strong, dedicated, bold!

Heaven must indeed be taken by violence!
With prayer your armor and good and
extraordinary works your battlepiece,
Rome shall be forced to look upon you
with benevolence

And crown you with glory as she did
(but ah! too few!)
Such women as Genevieve of Paris, Bridget,
Dorothy, and Bernice.

Dedicated to the Atlanta Council
of the National Council of Catholic Women.
Dr. Genevieve Jones, President

September 24, 1977

A LETTER TO PAUL

Where did you come from, my darling Paul?
Who scattered the gold dust that flecks
Your soul, and so enthralls me in your eyes?
Who, my charming spouse? Was it Mary,
In the *House of Gold?*

Who taught you how to love with so warm a
heart
And *Most Pure?*
To be *Most Amiable*, so humble, and yet
So wise?

Did you sit in the *Tower of Ivory*
And drink from her *Vessel of Honor?*

Did the *Mother of Christ*, and our own,
Plant the seed of your faith
Close beside the *Tower of David*
So it may grow and cling to its Cornerstone?

Was it the *Comforter of the Afflicted*
Who led you to care for the poor?
Was it the *Queen of Peace* who taught you
To be non-violent toward the wicked?

How did the *Queen of Virgins*
Teach you to respect women?
Was it the *Queen of All Saints*
Who insisted on self-restraint?

Where did you get that laugh? From the
Queen of Angels? Did she share one with you
As she watched her littlest angel
Chasing his halo down the golden stairs?

Did the *Mother Inviolate*, the *Mother Most*
Chaste,
Urge you to keep yourself inviolate,
Sacred for your marriage-bed?

Did she tell you that you and I, *together*,
Are the *Gate of Heaven* for each other?

And who made you so thoughtful of others,
So caring of the aged and the sick?
Was it the *Virgin Most Venerable?*
The *Health of the Sick?*

And did the *Singular Vessel of Devotion*
Inspire your extraordinary devotion
To Christ's most holy Church?

Today God sent us from afar
A baby girl, our *Mystical Rose.*
A girl—not a boy—
Fragile and beautiful and fragrant:
The result and the *Cause of our Joy,*
Our *Morning Star!*

Inspired by the *Litany of Loreto*

WOMEN THROUGHOUT THE AGES

The ancient Roman law
Considered women imbeciles (sic!)
Nomadic Jews, and huntsmen too,
Saw them as chattel
To be discarded at will.

The Greeks kept them
As childbearing slaves—
Secluded, unexercised, uneducated—
While male joy and pleasure
Was with courtesans and pretty boys.

In the fertile valley
Of the generous, timeless Nile
Men, however, stood in awe of women,
Symbolized them with a Mother-Goddess
And honored queens who ruled their land.

So, too, were women honored
At the waters of Babylon
Where the wise king, Hammurabi,
Made them independent
In the very first code of law.

In Judea, they bent
Like domesticated animals

Licking the hand of the master
Who fed them. And those causing conflict
Were banished to the desert—
Where they vanished, along with their Ishmaels.

Then Christ came down from the hills!

And filled their souls with hope . . .
For it was He
Who gave them dignity,
Extolling Mary's love of learning
Over her sister's burning complaint.
It was He
Who disdained to condemn women.
It was He
Who opposed men's right of disposal
And thwarted the law of Moses
By forbidding divorce.

Women of faith, scathed before,
Came forth in the Church
Singing hymns, calling for prayer,
Speaking in tongues, declaring prophecies.

When the men objected,
Paul boldly said:
"Do not quench the Spirit,
For He blows where He will . . .

There is neither male nor female.
You are all *one* in Christ."

But tradition was being upturned.
Soon Paul reverted
To the old ways, saying:
"Men! Uncover your heads!
You are the image of God!"

And he had the women interned
As if in a war, ordering them:
"Keep your heads covered!
Veil yourselves!
Keep silent in the Church!"

No doubt, he remembered
How, in the synagogue,
Women sat mute, darkly veiled,
Separated from men by screens opaque,
Nor dared to raise their voices.

Surely, it was Saul, not Paul—
Poor, suffering, charitable Paul—
Who denied women
The freedom Christ gave to all.

Thereafter—even to this day—
For centuries, Christianity crowned

Celibacy above marriage.
The Church Fathers viewed women as did the Jews:

They were the carriers
Of the stain of Eve;
They tempted men,
And even the saints fled from them.

And so they were locked into submission
By Paul—no! Saul, a Jew,
And Roman too,
Who ordained that state for women.

Neither men nor women
Witnessed the birth of the world—
Nor scientists,
Nor worthy men of God.

"You!" Woman now says
To those who would keep her down:
"You have divinized your own words!
You called woman Eve and Evil!"

Now she cries:

"No more! No more!
We were born to give life like man,
And like him, to do much more!
To live our own lives,
Since we have but one!
Since we have but one."

THE QUESTION

Unpredictable Life!
Pied Piper fife
On the 4th of July
With banners flying high!

Incomprehensible Life!
A Brutus-knife
In the agonized vein
Of bewildering pain.

God's familiar, unfamiliar metal
To test His creatures' mettle:
To shine with love and laughter;
Or to darken thereinafter

With hate and contraband
By their own hand . . .
Though He Himself engraved it
With one requisite or another.

Yet—besides their own—with every breath
From birth to death,
Other hands conjoin
To stencil this precious coin.

Now do I wonder:
If I—*alone*—were
Involved with Him,
What might have been

The marking—
Blazoning or blistering—
On an ensign
Of my very own design?

ABBA BABA

Who knows as well as these—
The speechless sick, the lonely bereaved,
The ones who hurt, and those captives
Of their own dripping eaves—
Who knows, better than these,
The loving, unbought kindness
Of this white-haired priest?

Ah, gleaming smile!
Like a gentling stream
You rise in his sheening eyes
Whose rippling joy is visible
To its source—that beautiful Faith—
Lying like a rock, immovable,
Embedded in that stream. Solid.

For a thousand nights and one,
He has entered my spacious cave.
The Church will come to you, he said
Long years ago when no longer could I go.

O Man of God, called Michael,
Did you know I called you
Ali Baba? Father Ali Baba?
Abba Baba! Ah, marvelous twist!

For you have—
For a thousand and one nights—
Discovered to me the Treasure of Heaven—
Its white gold, the Holy Eucharist.

And on each of those thousand nights,
I eagerly awaited the next
To hear your magic *Sesame*
That opened wide my heart . . .

The Body of Christ, Kay.

Celebrating, on May 25, 1991,
the 45th Anniversary
of the priesthood of
Monsignor Michael Regan

*ET HOMO FACTUS EST . . . PASSUS**
(and was made Man . . . suffered)

Out of a handful of dust,
The day before He rested,
The Lord made man and woman,
Then entrusted to them

The sheer joy of living—
As equals—
With the heavenly gifts
That He had given.

Among those blessings
Was the freedom of choice—
Free Will—and freedom
From pain which, then,
Had no name.

For God is Love
And Love is Joy,
And Joy knows no pain.

Oh, broken bodies!
Ah, hurting hearts!
Suffering does not abide
With God.

Yes, yes! Paradise
Was heaven on earth . . .
Until that filicidal day when,
Like a snake slithering
Into that delightful place,

Desire for a god's knowledge
Became the alloying fire that—
To the edge of unending time—
Burns with shame
The face of humankind.

From the moment of this default,
Tears yet sting the eyes
And scorch the throat of Woman,
Rise to scald the soul of Man.

Suffering became the mystery,
The enigma puzzling humanity
Muttering, *Why?*
Crying, *Why me?*

Forgetting

The compassion of our God
Who came down from Heaven
And became man in order
To walk in our shoes
And understand our pain . . .

To suffer with us
And die with us in exile
So that we may find again
Our way to Paradise.

Ah, Jesus!—
Him Whom the heavens
*Could not contain!***

*From the Nicene Creed, 325 A.D.
**From the First Lesson of Matins,
the Little Office of the
Blessed Virgin Mary.

The Most Reverend

James P. Lyke, O.F.M., Ph.D.

Archbishop of Atlanta

1991

THE GARDEN OF GETHSEMANE

gat shemanim

He presses his head
Against this most desolate rock,
Its fissures already reddened—
Centuries before—
By the Most Precious Blood
Of his most cherished Lord,

While the branches
Of the olive trees—
Forty feet high or more—
Tremble . . .
Remembering.

For the Most Reverend
James P. Lyke, O.F.M., Ph.D.
Archbishop of Atlanta

With earnest prayers
for your swift recovery,
and with love from me
and all your flock, assisted—
in the name of Christ—

by St. James the Just,
first Bishop of Jerusalem;
Sister Thea Bowman, Pierre Toussaint;
St. Francis of Assisi,
your father in Christ,
and the whole Court of the Saints
led by our Heavenly Queen.

May 28, 1992

GROWING OLD

Before we are born,
Before we escape into this
Windswept corridor through
The flume of our mother's womb,

Our Father—Lord
And Creator of all—
So that our thoughts may soar,
Fastened our wings with a special wax

Whose five chrisms we share
With all His creatures:
To taste, to smell, to hear,
To touch. And—most dear—to see . . .

Each sense providing animal pleasures
Most gratifying, yet taken
For granted by all who are human,
Who forget that it is the use of them

That is our weather-vane
Indicating the direction of our pain.

With oil spread on their feathers,
Through accident or self-pollution,
Some never raise their heads.

But others of us a sixth sense endows—
A sense of the spirit or just commonsense.

Oh, undeserved providence! when
Energetically we fly high and wide—
Like an eagle—into the sky . . .
Seeking the goal to be free
Of the shoals underneath while

Heeding the warning of red sky
At morning. But not of the setting sun
Whose blinding glare vandalizes us
Staring into its burning eye.

Then like those of Icarus,
Our wings fall off.

Down, down, down we plunge.
Suddenly we are all at sea—helpless—
And surely shall drown
Like the son of Daedalus.

But our Father is not like his father:
Take heart, we who are growing old!
God is walking on these waters—
We shall not drown like Icarus.

Faith supplies our feeble senses.*
We may flounder,
But we shall not drown.
God keeps us afloat

In this Aegean Sea until
Reaching for the hand of the Lord,
Our bodies wash up
On His eternal shore.

*Paraphrased
from the hymn
Pange Lingua
by St. Thomas Aquinas, O.P.
thirteenth century
Doctor of the Church

Runnymede Press

Founded 1992

Design by Kay Magenheimer

Artwork by James H. Couch

Afterword

Neither snow, nor rain, nor heat, nor gloom of night stays these couriers from the swift completion of their appointed rounds.[1]

Nor did my years, nor my blindness, nor various accidents and hospitalizations, nor a last minute inspiration that changed the format of this book—nor did the lack of a publisher—stay *First Light to Dawn* from finding a haven in your hands.

Like the English barons wresting the *Magna Carta* from their reluctant King John in 1215, I—after noting the swift passage of time at my age—declared myself free of continuing the time-consuming custom of "going the rounds of the trade publishers."

Thus, Runnymede Press was born in this year of 1992.

Thereafter, because of their 18 years' experience in the printing business, I turned to my niece, Betty, and her husband Samuel D. Couch, Sr., co-owners of CC Printing Company (804 Lake Connie Rd., Carrollton, Georgia 30117) and proposed that Runnymede Press become the book publishing division of their company.

The logo which I designed for Runnymede Press recalls the historic event that occurred in this meadow. It consists of a baron's shield traversed by a banner containing the date 1215. The upper portion reveals the reflection of the sun on the water of the Thames River. The lower portion depicts the

[1]Paraphrase, by William Mitchell Kendall, of the original Herodotus (Vol. VIII, Chap. 98). At the suggestion of Mr. Kendall, one of its architects, and with the permission of the Department of the U.S. Postal Service, this famous quotation was carved into the frieze of the facade of the General Post Office Building (1914) on 8th Avenue, New York City, to glorify the dedication of the letter carriers.

field Runnymede with its wild grasses and flowers. The initials MC (for *Magna Carta*) can be found by the discerning. The artist, James Couch, who executed this design is one of the six surviving sons of Betty and Sam. They also have two daughters, Cathy and Christine.

Obviously, *First Light to Dawn* does not contain my life's work, although there is one poem that dates from 1925. I was born in 1908, and I started writing poetry at age 13. (I was in love!) My mother gave me a room in our old homestead that I converted into a study. I have had one ever since.

The anticipation of going into my study lights up the beginning of my every day. It was at just such a beginning—staring into that eerie first light—that I was given the inspiration for the title and the organization of this book into three parts.

First Light (Part I) represents the development of one's initial perceptions of life. The word "dawn" is a metaphor for Christ, Whose teachings are deepened in the apperceiving of spiritual truths so long familiar. Hence, Part III is called *Dawn*.

The *Cloud of the Unknown* (Part II) is a metaphor for the mystery of lesbianism. To live always in the midst of inner conflict and outer intolerance, even hatred, is an ever deepening and transformative process. One seeks ceaselessly for spiritual peace in the face of the mystery which shrouds joy as well as pain. I believe—thanks be to God—I have found that peace.

I wish to thank the following people who by their encouragement or actual labors of love helped me produce this book:

Anne Collins;* Robert Moses,* internationally known builder of bridges, parks and parkways, who with Sidney Shapiro,* General Manager of the Long Island State Park

*Deceased

Commission, spent some Saturday mornings at a beach house at Gilgo reading my poems. I looked forward to Monday mornings when I received Mr. Moses' critical notes. Also Ambassador and former Senator Kenneth Keating,* and former Congressman Leo O'Brien,* a former colleague of mine on the Albany, New York *Times-Union*; former Congressman James R. Grover, Jr., of Babylon, NY, lifetime friend who helped me 30 years ago and still does. Also Msgr. James H. Casey,* Mother Adelaide, O.P.,* Jan Anderson (Zezima), former radio talk-host; John Bohannon and radio station WBAB of Babylon, NY. Also Robert Zittel, who wrote a term paper in the early sixties on my book *Love's Stigmata*, and Eileen Berg, who did the same ten years later at another college. Marianne Wolfe, former director of libraries in NY and Conn.

I am forever aware of Eleanor Roosevelt's gracious friendship which, beginning in 1932, lasted thirty years until her death in 1962. She was the indirect inspiration for many of my poems.

After 1968 I began to believe in the mystique of my relationship to the Kennedy's. I was being interviewed by a newspaper reporter on November 22, 1963, the date of the appearance of my first book, *Love's Stigmata*. In the midst of the interview, my sister, Betty Bennison, came to my door with the awesome news of the assassination of President John F. Kennedy.* The headlined story of this tragic event, in the local paper, contained the news of the publication of my book.

In 1968 I sent to Senator Robert F. Kennedy* a copy of my poetic tribute to Martin Luther King, Jr.,* and a copy of my poem *Ask Not . . .*, my tribute to the Senator's brother, which I had written on the date of his burial. Senator Kennedy replied immediately stating that he anticipated accepting personnally the engrossment of the poem for the John Fitzgerald Kennedy Library, which was built many years later at Columbia Point, Boston, MA. Robert was killed shortly before his campaign entourage was to have arrived in Long Island, NY, at which time there would have been an opportunity for me to make the presentation.

A year or two later, I had a letter from Rose Kennedy, the esteemed matriarch of the family, who confirmed the acceptance of *Ask Not . . .* for the Kennedy Library, which was still in the planning stage. I appreciate her kindness to me, especially since she wrote this letter during the final illness of her husband, Joseph.

The engrossment of *Ask Not . . .* was finally accessioned and catalogued by Dave Powers, Museum Curator at the JFK Library, in 1991.

Thank you also to the United States Government for including this poem in its book *John Fitzgerld Kennedy, Late a President of the United States.*

And to Richard Cardinal Cushing,* Archbishop of Boston and great friend of the Kennedy family, who sent me the picture of President Kennedy which appears in this book. The cardinal's autograph appears on the picture.

I am most grateful to Sister M. Rose de Lima Moran, R.S.M., who sent an unknown number of *Love's Stigmata* to prestigious libraries throughout Europe and South America. Also for their prayers and other favors to Sister John Michael Horgan, O.P., Sister Mary Alice Fritz, O.P., both of Amityville, NY. Also to Winifred C. McNamee of Florida for prayers and necessary dates. Also to Floyd McGlone of Babylon for his efforts to furnish me with a necessary name.

Also my deepest thanks to Jeannette Dolny, now of Florida. She was District Director of the Business and Professional Women's Clubs of Nassau and Suffolk Counties, L.I., NY, and, later, Chair of the (New York) State Foundation. She was a fellow-member of my B&PW Club in Bay Shore, NY. Her support has been constant over the years.

Also to my faithful friend Nathan Ballin of Brightwaters,

NY, who was my colleaque at LISPC; and also my very spiritual friend and fellow Babylonian, Marie Stehle.

Also for encouraging words from Pope Paul VI* and Pope John Paul II through the Vatican Secretariat of State. My poems for them are in their archives.

Also my appreciation for the inclusion of my poems, for them, in the following presidential archives or libraries: Harry S Truman,* Dwight D. Eisenhower,* Lyndon B. Johnson,* Richard M. Nixon, and Jimmy Carter.

It is an honor to acknowledge the irresistible letter from Sister Mary Luke Tobin, S.L., Director of the Thomas Merton Center for Creative Exchange, Denver, CO. She was the only female Religious from the United States who attended Vatican II as an Auditor.

Thanks too to Sister Sandra M. Schneiders, I.H.M., renowned New Testament scholar and associate professor of New Testament studies and Christian spirituality at the Jesuit School of Theology at Berkeley, CA, for her strong belief in the importance of the imagination in religious experience and the ways in which the imagination is formed. "Since you are a poet," she wrote, "I am not surprised that you understood well what I was trying to say . . . ."

When I retired and moved to the South, I found many friends who for the past 17 years also have been encouraging and helpful. I give my deepest gratitude to Dr. Virginia M. Meehan, now Professor of English Emerita at West Georgia College, and my friend and companion for many years, who introduced me to many of these people and who herself took a personal interest in my writing.

Also to Claudette Hayes, M.D., who upon the publication of my inaugural poem for President Jimmy Carter, hosted a dinner party at her home in my honor.

I am indebted to the Rev. R. Gregg Kaufman, founding pastor of Grace Lutheran Church in Carrollton, for his invitation to write a poem for its dedication. I attended the dedication with Dr. Virginia Meehan, and we were the only Catholics at that event.

Also to Ken Childs, newscaster of radio station WLBB of Carrollton, GA and to Jerry Mock, Director of Learning Resources Center and formerly at WWGC.

To Sandra Aylesworth, my neighbor.

Also to Dianne Smith for her initial help.

Also to Dr. William S. Doxey, Jr., Professor of English at West Georgia College, for his visible enthusiasm and his favorable critical reaction to my poetry, which produced the crucial spark to my determination to publish *First Light to Dawn*.

To Sadie Hughes from Bremen.

To Martha Setter, for her encouragement and help so necessary, and to her husband Henry for the use of a picture of his sculpture, *Seat of Wisdom*.

Also to Mary Sanders, without whom my bills would remain unpaid, and to Jimmy, her husband, who continues to do many necessary errands for me in Atlanta. Also to their daughter, Amy Carlson, for some typing.

To Frank Herron, my neighbor who with his wife, Virginia, became my friends through this book. Frank is a witty humorist and a waggish punster. He has given me the rare opportunity to see creativity at work. Inexpressible thanks to you, Frank, for the many, many *long hours* you spent proofreading the galleys.

Also to Elizabeth Mathews (whom I call "Liz the Whiz" because of her incredible speed and accuracy) for exceedingly *long* hours proofreading.

Many thanks to Sally Grubbs, secretary to Archbishop Lyke of Atlanta, for sending to me his picture for use in this book.

Also to (Mrs. Grady) Pat Dickson, parish secretary for Our Lady of Perpetual Help Church, Carrollton, for her research of church files for necessary data.

To Bruce Bobick, chairman of the Art Dept., West Georgia College, for his cooperation.

To Clois Reece, my typist, to whom I am most grateful for the finished manuscript.

My blessings on Lunell Addison, my housekeeper, who not only keeps my house immaculate but also keeps me in good humor all the time, and especially during the stress of the preparation of this book.

To my niece, Betty, and her husband, my godson Sam Couch, my profround gratitude for providing the parent company for Runnymede Press and the skills and printing experience responsible for the beauty and fine quality of this book.

I am most grateful to Dr. Brenda Fitzgerald, FACOG, who to my delight told me the day after her Primary defeat that she will continue to run for a seat in the U.S. House of Representatives. Her favor to me—at that time, a stranger to her—is most appreciated. A phone call to her settled a controversial poem from a physiological viewpoint. This is the poem that created such an enthusiastic response in Sister Mary Luke Tobin, S.L. Thank you, Brenda, and I hope that you will eventually find your way around the Halls of Congress.

I also give my everlasting thanks to Monsignor Michael J. Regan, J.C.D., Pastor of Our Lady of Perpetual Help Church in Carrollton, GA, and my dear friend who allowed me to tap his enormous storehouse of knowledge.

And to the Fourth Degree Knights of Columbus members of the Jonesboro Assembly, who honored me with a plaque in recognition of my poetry.

There are no words to describe the patience, kindness and invaluable help given me over the telephone by Mr. Bernard C. Dietz, Head of the Renewal Section of the Copyright Office in Washington, D.C. Not only did he give me most important assistance and advice, but also put me in touch with his longtime friend, Ed Komen, the attorney in Washington, who searched out the availability of the name Runnymede Press and reported the name clear for my use in the United States and England. While I was still on a formal basis with Mr. Dietz, Ed Komen told me that a more even-tempered man does not exist. And it is true. Bernie (you see, we have since become friends) is a most consistently sweet-tempered man. His voice bespeaks a most friendly nature. I call his work-a-day voice "a voice with a smile in it." My heartfelt thanks to you, Bernie, for your graciousness and your practical help; and to you too, Ed, for helping me in the foundation of Runnymede Press. You both were most generous.

Also thanks to the employees of AT&T; both domestic long distance and overseas personnel deserve the public expression of my appreciation of their warmth and kindness when they learned I was a blind person dependent on them for their help. AT&T can be proud of them! Not one of them failed me. Thank you, dear unknown friends.

To my very dear and endearing friend Charles Beard, Director of Ingram Library at West Georgia College and immediate Past Co-Chair of the Taskforce for the White House Conference on Library and Information Services, for his generosity in giving his personal attention to certain of my requests. Also to Jan Ruskell, Head of Reference, and her staff—Myron House and Joanne Artz—for their invaluable assistance.

My thanks to Rev. Dr. Brantley Harwell, former pastor of the First Baptist Church, Carrollton, GA, and now pastor of the First Baptist Church in Morrow, GA, for his generous recognition of my talent.

Many thanks to Dr. Tracy Stallings, Director of College Relations at West Georgia College, and longtime Mayor of the City of Carrollton, for his generous public recognition of my gift.

Also to Mrs. Billie Turner, Assistant Vice President and Corporate Secretary of the former Peoples Bank in Carrollton. She was the most gracious hostess at the bank's exhibition of the engrossment of my poem *Born Again*, after which it was sent, as an inaugural gift, to President Jimmy Carter at the White House. It was at that time that I first met Congressman Newt Gingrich who, then a candidate for election, stopped at the bank to have his picture taken with me. He is now the Republican Whip of the House of Representatives.

To JoAnn Yeager Adkins, of Atlanta, editor of the *Reach of Song*, a collection of members' poems published annually by the Georgia State Poetry Society, and to Edward Davin Vickers,* founding President of GSPS, for their beautiful friendship and support.

To Elizabeth Harris, former First Lady of Georgia, my thanks for her most gracious letter and her kind words about my first two books of poetry, which had been accepted by her for the library in the Governor's Mansion at a GSPS luncheon in her honor.

To Leona Mucheck, of Villa Rica, my gratitude for her instant response in an emergency connected with this book.

And now thinking back some thirty years, my first real encouragement came from Ken McCormick, then Editor-in-Chief (and now Emeritus) of Doubleday.

My gratitude to Jack Carter, Postmaster, Carrollton, GA, for his quick response to my request for the wording of the famous postal quotation which serves as the introduction to this Afterword. Also for the information in the footnote.

My deepest appreciation to the James Cooper's (father* and son) *Babylon Leader*, and its successor, Ed* & Jane Wolfe's *The Beacon*, also to the *Amityville Record*, *Islip Press*, and *Smithtown Messenger*, who introduced my first book *Love's Stigmata* and some later poems to my Northern readers. So too Stanley Parkman's newspapers introduced me to my Southern readers. His papers deserving public thanks were the *Carroll County Georgian* which, consolidated with the *Times-Free Press*, evolved into the *Daily Times-Georgian* and then into the *Times-Georgian*. Also I thank the short-term and now defunct *West Georgia News*. Also *Our Lady's Parish Happenings*.

I am deeply indebted to all of you, including the Parkman quartet: Andy Bowen, Frances Long, Hiram Bray, and Bill Fordham. Each of you treated me with the utmost Southern courtesy during my now 17 years' residency here. Thank you most heartily, Frances, Andy, Hiram, and Bill.

Also, my gratitude to the official publication of the Archdiocese of Atlanta, *The Georgia Bulletin*, and its editor, Gretchen R. Keiser.

And a most special thank you to my dear and beloved friend, Barb Tervo, who being a poet herself, shares my love of poetry. And of God. She has been with me in this preparation of the manuscript from the beginning and is even now—after midnight—helping me with it at the end. Barb, I love you for being you. I am grateful for your intelligent help.

Indeed, all my expressions of gratitude in this Afterword are *special*! I hope the following volunteers—whose combined labor rewarded me with a Rolodex file of at least 1,500 names and addresses of longtime and prospective readers—will remember how very grateful I am to them for their help. This was the most worrisome task of all and the most humble yet it was not beneath the dignity of these splendid friends and citizens of Carroll County. Most sincere thanks then to the following who came back to my home time and time again until the job was completed by the deadline: Mary Sanders, Martha Setter, Elizabeth Mathews, Betty Griffth, Eileen Frykman, Anna Fazio, and Christine Couch; also Nellie Duke, who was recently appointed to the Georgia State Commission on Women. Also to Mary Miles, M.D., Caroline Blumenthal, and Clare Doherty. Also to Alice Richards, the beloved matriarch of the family of the late Roy Richards, Sr., the founder of Southwire Company, the largest independent producer of wire and cable in the world. She is also an invaluable member of Southwire's *Education Initiative Program* whereby Southwire funds school projects over a seven-county area.

In the above mentioned group is the prominent Carrollton businessman Jimmy Sanders, president of Batey & Sanders, Inc. suppliers of heavy equipment parts. Also, William Carter Deegan, and Steve Dembowski.

Also in that group are the following eminent men: Dr. Ward Pafford, President-Emeritus of West Georgia College, Dr. Richard Dangle, recently retired Professor of Physics and Dean of Arts and Sciences at WGC, Dr. James W. Mathews, recently retired Professor of English and Chair of the English Department at WGC, and Dr. Paul Hull Bowdre, Jr., WGC Professor of English Emeritus. Lamar Plunkett, founder and Chairman-Emeritus of Lamar Manufacturing Company and Bowdon Manufacturing Company, manufacturers of men's and women's tailored clothing.

Not only for the above task, but also—again!—for reasons an author understandably appreciates, I heartily thank Stanley Parkman, founder and Publisher-Emeritus of the *Times-Georgian*, Carrollton, Georgia.

Now we come to the great triumvirate without whose dedicated friendship and extreme generosity these poems may never have been enjoyed by you.

First, I must mention my nephew's wife, Delores Baker Bennison, who drove down from Long Island, NY, to spend a week with me here in Carrollton to assist in the organization of this book. We worked for five consecutive days, sometimes forgetting meals. She brought her own electric typewriter from the North. Her organization of my manuscript is the most admirable possible. Thank you, Delores.

And Mary Anne Wilson Goreau de Villier, editor *par excellence* and most faithful friend, who despite a certain frailty in her delicate nature was at my side through the thick and thin of this book: advising, chasing commas, ellipses, and all gremlins that would dilute the meaning of these poems. *Jessica*, how can I thank you? You are, indeed, a most reliable friend. *Merci beaucoup, ma charmamte amie!*

And beyond my wildest dreams is the Foreword written by my friend, *most dear*, Eugenia Price, who, with my letter in hand, called me from her home on St. Simons Island to order five books as gifts for her friends.

Eugenia Price is known here and abroad as the author of 37 historical novels and spiritual books, and is about to complete the *Georgia Trilogy* for Doubleday. The first book of this trilogy, *Bright Captivity*, has been on the *New York Times* best seller list.

Genie, readers illumed by your distinguished Foreword are bound to be interested in this book. For your exquisite kindness, and deep concern for me, your "beloved" friend and fellow writer, thank you with all my heart. *With all my heart!*

Lastly, but most importantly, I give thanks to God, Creator and Lord of all, for His love and generosity toward me. He has graced me with a loving and supportive family and longtime magnificent friends. Also 16 godchildren!

It was He Who endowed me with the gift of poesy. With this gift and the gifts of my Faith, my health, and my other talents, my life has been *most joyous and most wonderful*. Thank You, dear God.

Kay Magenheimer
Carrollton, Georgia

September 19, 1992